Alfred Williams Momerie

Agnosticism

Alfred Williams Momerie

Agnosticism

ISBN/EAN: 9783743382022

Manufactured in Europe, USA, Canada, Australia, Japa

Cover: Foto ©Lupo / pixelio.de

Manufactured and distributed by brebook publishing software (www.brebook.com)

Alfred Williams Momerie

Agnosticism

AGNOSTICISM

"Truth is the property of God; the pursuit of Truth is what belongs to Man."
—*Von Müller.*

AGNOSTICISM

Sermons Preached in St Peter's, Cranley Gardens, 1883-4

BY

ALFRED WILLIAMS MOMERIE
M.A., D.SC., LL.D.

LATE FELLOW OF ST JOHN'S COLLEGE, CAMBRIDGE;
PROFESSOR OF LOGIC AND METAPHYSICS
IN KING'S COLLEGE, LONDON

FOURTH EDITION, REVISED

WILLIAM BLACKWOOD AND SONS
EDINBURGH AND LONDON
MDCCCXCI

CONTENTS.

PART I.

DISBELIEF IN GOD: AS EXEMPLIFIED BY MODERN THINKERS.

		PAGE
I.	THE EXISTENCE OF THE SOUL,	3
II.	THE EXISTENCE OF THE SOUL (*continued*),	18
III.	THE SOUL'S KNOWLEDGE OF ITSELF,	32
IV.	IMMORTALITY,	47
V.	EVOLUTION OF SPECIES,	62
VI.	EVOLUTION OF THE ANIMAL AND VEGETABLE KINGDOMS,	77
VII.	EVOLUTION OF LIFE,	90
VIII.	EVOLUTION OF WORLDS,	103
IX.	CONSCIOUSNESS,	119
X.	PURPOSE *VERSUS* CHANCE,	134
XI.	THE INFINITE MIND,	148

Agnosticism.

I.

THE EXISTENCE OF THE SOUL.

A LARGE class of modern thinkers tell us that we have not, and cannot have, any knowledge of God. Let us examine this doctrine of Agnosticism. If it be true, faith is a mistake; prayer is a mockery; to hope for immortality is as unreasonable as to hope for wings. Nothing worth calling a religion, as we saw last Advent,[1] can ever be founded upon an agnostic basis. And as for Christianity, well—if the agnostics are right—no one was ever the victim of more serious delusions than Jesus Christ of Nazareth.

The word "agnostic" was invented about

---

[1] See my 'Basis of Religion,' *passim*, and two sermons on "Our right to Immortality," in my 'Preaching and Hearing; and other Sermons.'

twenty years ago by Professor Huxley, and means —one who does not know. It is the exact opposite of gnostic, the prefix *a* in Greek having a negative signification. In the first few centuries of the Christian era there were various sects of philosophers, who went under the general name of gnostics, and who all agreed in asserting that they knew a great deal about the mysteries of existence, and in particular about the nature of God and the method of Creation. For instance, there was the system of the Basilidians. In this system the Deity is said to be connected with the visible and material world by a long series of emanations. From the divine essence were evolved beings called Mind, Reason, Intellect, Wisdom, Power, Justice, and Peace; and they, together with the divine essence, constituted the first scale of existence and inherited the highest heaven. These primary emanations of the Deity produced other less ethereal emanations, which in their turn again produced others still less ethereal. Altogether there were three hundred and sixty-five emanations, and each of them had a realm or sphere in which it reigned supreme. The lowest of these spheres, the three hundred and sixty-fifth, bordered on the realm of matter; and it was the chief archon or ruler of this lowest intellectual sphere, who reduced the original chaos of matter to order, and so became the Creator of what we call the world. All this is worked out in the system of the Basilidians, with as much minuteness of detail as if the description were the work of an eyewitness. Now it is, as I said, the extreme opposite of such gnosticism which is signified by the term agnosticism. An agnostic is one who declares that he knows nothing—absolutely nothing—of the nature of God or of any kindred subject. There may be a God, for anything that agnosticism has to say to the contrary. It simply asserts that we cannot, from the very nature of our faculties, ever hope to know whether there be a God or not.

The spread of agnosticism in the present day is, I suppose, a fact which has been recognised by all of you. While the lower classes are inclined to atheism, the more cultivated members of the community are, in large numbers, declaring themselves agnostics. No one, of course, but a very ignorant and stupid person could ever be a dogmatic atheist. The man who *denies* the existence of God virtually asserts his own divinity; for he implies that he has been everywhere and seen everything, and that nothing can exist in an infinite universe which *he* has failed to detect. Agnosticism, on the other hand, at first sight seems to be but the natural outcome of that humble sense of ignorance, which ever increases with the increase of knowledge. It is the creed of a large number of illustrious scientists, such as Tyndall and Huxley. It seems to have been at times the creed of the late Charles Darwin. I daresay most of you saw in the papers some time ago a copy of an interesting letter sent by Darwin to a Mr Fordyce, who had defended the philosopher from the charge of atheism, and had written to ask if he was right in so doing. "It seems to me absurd to doubt," wrote Darwin, "that a man may be an ardent theist and an evolutionist. . . . What my own views may be, is a question of no consequence to any one except myself. But as you ask, I may state that my judgment often fluctuates. In my most extreme fluctuations I have never been an atheist, in the sense of denying the existence of a God. I think that generally, and more and more as I grow older, but not always, an agnostic would be the most correct description of my state of mind." And agnosticism is not only the creed of some of the most brilliant scientific teachers; it is being adopted by many of the most promising learners. The teachers of science do not always confine themselves, as Darwin did, to their own proper subjects; they sometimes go out of their way to discuss metaphysical questions, upon which—being non-experts—they have no authoritative voice. Their disciples often fail to perceive this distinction. They often fail to recognise the simple fact that a good scientist may be a bad metaphysician. And so, along with the excellent science of the agnostics, the student frequently adopts, almost as a matter of course, their wretched metaphysics, and becomes an agnostic himself. It is in this way that agnosticism is spreading among persons of average, or more than average, intellect.

Of course there is a large number of persons who are not influenced by agnosticism. There are a great many people in our own and other Churches who never read, with the exception of third-rate novels and the newspaper; who never think, except as to how they can make or spend money; who never even hear what is going on in the world of thought. They have inherited their creed, just like their estate, from their ancestors; and the former has in their eyes this great advantage over the latter—it does not require any looking after. As for investigating it, or testing it in the light of modern thought, they would as soon think of examining their own brains. These persons are saved from the risk of going wrong by never making any attempt to go right. They avoid error by not seeking truth. They are uninfluenced by agnosticism, simply because they never enter into the intellectual region where agnosticism is to be found.

But there is a still larger number of persons, and the number is continually increasing, who do read and think; who are determined, so far as in them lies, to believe only what is true; and who are convinced that a theological creed can be of no value, unless it harmonises with the ascertained facts of science. It is such persons as these who are adopting, or are in danger of adopting, the agnostic creed. Those of them upon whom the lessons of childhood made the deepest impression may still cling—agnosticism notwithstanding—cling with the very energy of despair to their early faith. But they are every now and then pained, embarrassed, staggered, by the fact that so many of their intellectual superiors consider their faith to be absurd. The spirit of agnosticism is in the air. The reviews are full of it. Popular lecturers are everywhere insisting upon it. We meet it in novels, and even in poetry. At the universities it is the predominant creed among the undergraduates and the younger dons. And, worst of all, we hear it sometimes in drawing-rooms from women's lips—from women, strange to say, who are young and fair, who are, or should be, happy. It will be worth our while, then, to examine this creed, and see if it really deserves the wide and ready acceptance it has received.

Professor Huxley, in a passage which is often quoted, gives rather a misleading account of the doctrine. "Agnosticism," he says, "is of the essence of science, whether ancient or modern. It simply means that a man shall not say he knows or believes what he has no scientific ground for professing to know or believe." Now that is a definition of honesty. In that sense we ought all to be agnostics.

But agnosticism, in point of fact, goes on to specify certain objects, regarding which it asserts that we *never can* have any scientific ground for belief. One of these objects is the Deity. Of the Deity the agnostic asserts, not merely that he knows nothing, but that nothing can be known. And it is not of God alone that the agnostics maintain we must necessarily be ignorant. They base the inability to know God upon a more general inability—the inability, namely, to know anything but *phenomena*. The word "phenomenon," in scientific discussions, does not mean, as in common parlance, something remarkable or uncommon. Etymologically it signifies that which appears; and its scientific signification is in keeping with its etymology. It stands in science for anything that appears in consciousness, either as sensation or as thought. Now the agnostics tell us—*and this is the essence of agnosticism*—that consciousness is entirely resolvable into phenomena or appearances; that it is nothing more than a series of sensations and thoughts. My consciousness at any moment, they say, is just the sensation or the thought which I happen to be at that moment experiencing. My consciousness, considered as a whole, is the entire number of sensations and thoughts which I experience during my lifetime. I exist one instant as a state of sensation, another instant as a state of thought; now I am a feeling of pleasure, and anon a feeling of pain: at this moment I am thinking of, or am the thought of, one object; a little while ago I was thinking of, or was the thought of, another object. Taking my whole life into account, I am just the sum total of these sensations and thoughts, the entire series of my varied experiences. There is nothing underlying my sensations and thoughts, which remains identical while they change and pass away. I am, not myself, but my experiences. In other words, I have no soul.[1] You will bear in mind, of course, that a genuine agnostic does not dogmatically deny the existence of the soul, but only the possibility of knowing it. He would say,—I may have a soul; I may have dozens of souls, for anything I know to the contrary. But what he insists upon is this, that the soul is neither given nor implied in our experience; that sensations and thoughts, which are ever changing and passing away, make up the whole of our conscious life—constitute, so far as we know, our entire being.

Now if it can be shown that the agnostics are wrong about the soul, it will follow that they are wrong in their general principles. If we can be sure of the existence of the soul, it will follow that knowledge is not confined to phenomena. For the soul, if a soul there be, is neither a passing sensation nor a passing thought, nor is it a collection of passing sensations and thoughts.

---

[1] For the sake of the non-philosophical reader, I had better mention that the terms ego, self, soul, mind, and personality are synonyms.

It is a single, permanent something, underlying and outlasting these transitory phenomena.

That the agnostics are wrong, it is not at all difficult to show. It is the very irony of fate, that persons holding such a profoundly absurd doctrine as the non-existence of a soul, should have been induced to call themselves " exact thinkers." If by chance there is any one here this afternoon, who has never come across books like those of James Mill, or John Stuart Mill, or Tyndall, or Huxley, he will probably imagine I am wasting my time in combating a theory, which men in their sober senses never could have held. And yet, in point of fact, this theory is adopted at the present moment by not a few of the very ablest scientists. It behoves us therefore, as I have said, to examine the doctrine with care.

And in this examination I am happy to be able to follow the advice of my opponents—the so-called exact thinkers. They are always warning us to beware of the misleading influence of language. They remind us of Hobbes's maxim, that words are the coins of wise men, but the money of fools. They tell us that we, and other foolish persons like ourselves, who believe in God and the soul, have a stupid way of fancying that existence must agree with language, that words necessarily imply actual objects corresponding to them: whereas language, if translated into thought, is often found to be inaccurate; and thought, if compared with actual existence, frequently turns out to be untrue. Their advice is good. For all purposes of exact thinking, it is necessary to translate language into thought, and to compare thought with existence.

Let us now, bearing this in mind, do a little piece of exact thinking on our own account. Let us analyse carefully the meaning of the words phenomenon, appearance, sensation, thought. If we do so, we shall find that it is our opponents —the agnostics—who have been misled by language, and who have been guilty of hasty, careless, inaccurate thinking. They have assumed that because in each case the word is single, the corresponding object in existence must be likewise single. But a very little reflection may suffice to show that these single words stand for double facts. Appearances, thoughts, feelings cannot exist by themselves. They can exist only in a mind or soul. An appearance, in order that it may be an appearance, must appear to some one. A feeling, in order that it may be a feeling, must be felt by some one. A thought, in order that it may be a thought, must be thought by some one. Descartes said, "I think, therefore I am. It is necessary that I who think should be somewhat." But we may go a step further than Descartes. We may say, —I feel, therefore I am. It is necessary that I who feel should be somewhat. If I have a feeling, I must exist to have it. It is as true of sensation as of thought, that it involves the existence of what in philosophical language is termed the ego, of what is popularly called the soul. Just as a thought means something thought by some one, so a feeling means something felt by some one. Without the some one to think, the something could not be thought. Without the some one to feel, the something could not be felt. Since, then, without a soul there could be no feelings, it is absurd to deny or to ignore the existence of the soul because it cannot itself be felt. You might as reasonably maintain that sensations do not exist because they are not souls, as that souls do not exist because they are not sensations. The existence of the soul is involved in the existence of the sensation; and if you can be sure of the reality of the one, you can be equally sure of the reality of the other.

Perhaps the agnostic, when hard pressed in

this way, may feel himself obliged to admit that the single word sensation does really stand for something double; and he may even allow us, if we please, to apply the term "soul" to one of the elements in this complex fact. But now he will insist upon it that this soul is not permanent, that it is no more permanent than the feelings and the thoughts with which it correlates. Granting, he will say, that the phenomenon involves two elements, both elements pass away together. Allowing that the soul exists, there is no proof that it *persists*. Is there not? Let us do another little piece of exact thinking. Let us analyse the meaning of the word remembrance.

Just as sensation involves the feeling felt and the mind or soul which feels, so a remembrance involves the fact remembered and the mind or soul which remembers. But a third element is also involved in every act of remembrance— namely, the soul's consciousness or recognition of its permanence. Let us take an illustration. I remember that some years ago many of my opinions were changed by the reading of a certain book. Now this implies, (1) The object or fact remembered—namely, the change of my opinions by the perusal of the book. (2) My soul or mind, which remembers the fact, or which, as we sometimes say, has the remembrance. And (3) a consciousness of personal identity; that is to say, a conviction that the mind or soul which is now experiencing the remembrance of the fact, is the self-same mind or soul which formerly experienced the fact itself—that it is, in other words, *my* mind. The identity of which I am conscious, is certainly not an identity of body, for during the years which have elapsed my body has lost its identity. Nor is the identity an identity of phenomena, for the remembrance of the fact is something essentially different from the fact itself. The identity of which I am conscious is an identity of soul. I am sure, I know, that I, who am now remembering a certain change of opinions, once actually experienced the change; and that in the meantime I, one and the self-same subject, a single, indivisible, permanent being, have been apprehending sensations, and thinking thoughts, and remembering events, and gathering up these varied experiences into the unity of a personal life. Without a permanent or persistent soul there could be no memory; for it is just the recognition of this permanence, which is the characteristic feature of every act of remembrance. This you will see more clearly, perhaps, by contrasting remembrance with imagination. I may imagine my opinions being changed in certain ways some years hence. But here no knowledge of persistence is involved; because I am not sure that my opinions will be so changed: in other words, I am not sure that I shall ever exist in the particular state I am imagining. But in remembrance I perceive that I, who am now recollecting, did actually exist in a different state, of which the present remembrance is only a representation. In other words, in every act of remembrance I know that I have existed in at least two different states, and that therefore I have *persisted* between them.[1]

Thus you see by a little careful analysis—the "exact thinkers" notwithstanding—it is possible to demonstrate the existence of a soul. Exact thinkers! Why, I tell you, in the whole history of human thought, there are no grosser instances of slipshod reasonings and patent fallacies, than those by which the so-called exact thinkers have sought to rid us of our souls!

---

[1] Of course this argument applies also to the lower animals. The difference between men and brutes is only a difference of faculty or development.

Agnosticism.

II.

THE EXISTENCE OF THE SOUL.—*Continued.*

ACCORDING to the fundamental assumption of the agnostics, as we have seen, all knowledge is restricted to phenomena—that is to say, to the transitory sensations and thoughts which are constantly appearing in consciousness, and as constantly passing away. We ourselves are merely a series of such passing phenomena, merely the sum total of our conscious experiences. There is in us no permanent, persistent mind, underlying and outlasting our changing states; in other words, we have no souls. Now we saw that this theory of consciousness was thoroughly and absurdly incorrect. We saw that the existence of the soul was implied in the very meaning of the term sensation, which single word stands for a double fact, signifying something felt by some one. Since there can be no such thing as an unfelt feeling, and since, without the soul to feel, the feeling would be unfelt, it follows that the existence of the soul is the essential condition of the existence of sensation. And the permanence or persistence of this soul, as distinguished from the transitoriness of phenomena, is proved to us, as I pointed out, in every act of remembrance. Since the fact, and the remembrance of the fact, are separated from each other by a certain interval of time, and since, in recollection, we are conscious of having been present to both, it follows that we must have retained our identity in the meanwhile; it follows, in other words, that while our sensations and thoughts merely *exist*, we ourselves *persist*.

During the week I received a letter, which may very probably give expression to thoughts that existed in other minds besides the writer's. My correspondent says: "With reference to your sermon yesterday afternoon, may I be excused for writing to say, that the arguments you then used to prove the existence of the soul did not seem to me sufficient,—for this reason: By the word 'soul' I understand something which not only exists and persists in man, but something which always so persists, even when the flesh-wrappings have dissolved. And you, to my thinking, only proved the persistence of something during life, which I think not even an agnostic would care to refute. Could you kindly carry the argument on this point further, I, and I believe many members of your congregation, would be extremely obliged."

Now the receipt of this note has suggested to me, that I had better spend somewhat more time than I had originally intended to do, in discussing the existence of the soul. The subject is so very fundamental, and there is so much which yet remains to be said, that I think it would be unwise to hurry over it. "Man, know thyself," says Pope; "all wisdom centres there." Unless we can be sure of the existence of the soul, we can never be sure of the existence of God. Unless we can know something of the nature of the soul, we can never know anything of the nature of God. And, conversely, a complete knowledge of the soul would be a complete knowledge of God,—as complete, at least, as was possible for a finite intellect. I think it was St Chrysostom who said, "He who truly knows himself, knows God." So that if we spend our time this Advent in trying to ascertain what may be known about the soul, we shall be in a better position for ascertaining on a future occasion what may be known about God.

My correspondent is quite right in saying that I did not, last Sunday, prove the existence of the soul in his sense of the word; I did not prove the existence of an immortal soul. I purposely omitted all reference to immortality, intending to refer to it in a sentence or two later on. In consequence of this letter, however, I shall devote an entire sermon to the subject. The questions as to the existence of the soul and the immortality of the soul are totally distinct; they must be argued on completely different grounds; and it is most important that we should keep them carefully separated in our thoughts. My correspondent's definition of the word soul is an arbitrary definition, telling us what *he* means by the term, but not what is generally or necessarily meant by it. No doubt to a Christian the word soul suggests the idea of immortality; but it did not do so to a Jew, it does not do so to a Buddhist. The Jews were pre-eminently believers in the soul; they regarded it as the very breath of Jehovah. And yet, with few and rare exceptions, they thought that life ended with the grave. "To go hence" meant with them "to be no more." The next world was to them "the land of forgetfulness." The Buddhists, too, believe in a soul—in a soul which persists, in spite of death, through a large number of transmigrations: and yet it is not, they think, destined to be immortal; the ultimate end of it is Nirvana or unconsciousness—that is to say, extinction. So that you see the idea of the soul does not necessarily involve the idea of immortality. The existence of the soul is one thing; its duration is manifestly another. To discuss the immortality of the soul, without having settled its existence, would be like attempting to describe the inhabitants of the planet Mars, before we were quite sure that there were any.

The positive bearing of the remarks which I made last Sunday on the doctrine of immortality, I shall point out by-and-by. Their negative bearing must be already evident. Unless what I then said were true, immortality would be impossible, for the simple reason that there is, in that case, nothing to be immortal. A thing must exist in order to possess any given quality. The existence of the soul in my sense—in the general sense of the word—is the *sine quâ non* to its existence in my correspondent's sense. If

I be resolvable into sensations and thoughts, if I be indistinguishable from my passing experiences, then *I*, in the proper sense of the word, do not exist at all; and not existing now, I cannot of course continue to exist for ever.

I must beg leave to differ from my correspondent when he says the persistence of the soul, which I attempted last Sunday to prove, is a persistence which agnostics would not think it worth while to refute. For in the first place they do in point of fact refute, or endeavour to refute it. And in the second place there is a very plain reason why they should look upon its refutation as important. True, the soul of which I then spoke need not necessarily be immortal. True, the persistence I then tried to demonstrate was only the persistence which is implied in memory; and memory, for anything I have yet said, may cease at death. But the soul with which I have been so far concerned, though not *primâ facie* immortal, is to say the least *noumenal*, and therefore contradicts the fundamental doctrine of the agnostic philosophy—the doctrine, namely, that knowledge is restricted to phenomena. The word noumenon is the technical term in philosophy for that which underlies and outlasts phenomena. That which persists is called a noumenon, to indicate that it is not apprehensible by the senses, but only by the reason (νοῦς). We have seen that the process of recollection involves, in addition to sensations and thoughts which pass away, the existence of something which remains. Now the something that remains, if it remain but for an hour, is a noumenal existence, no less than if it remained for ever. It is not on the ground of its persisting for a longer or shorter time that the soul is denied by the agnostics, but on the ground of its persisting at all. Our knowledge, they tell us, is necessarily confined to sensations and thoughts which do *not* persist. If, then, it can be shown that we know something of a soul which does persist, no matter how ephemerally, the very foundation of agnosticism is destroyed.

Now what I wanted to make plain to you last Sunday was this. Using the term soul, not in the Christian sense of an immortal being, but in the general and philosophical sense of a being which persists and remains identical while its sensations change,—using the term soul in this sense, the agnostic doctrine of its non-existence is untenable and absurd.

The fallacies by which it is supported would scarcely have convinced any one, but for their being broached by eminent and illustrious men. A great name is constantly mistaken for a great argument. Here we have a simple explanation of the fact that the agnostic doctrines are being so readily and widely received. That the authors of these fallacies should have been themselves imposed on, is rather more difficult to understand. We may feel better satisfied, perhaps, in differing from them, if we see what it is that has led them wrong. On this point I will offer two remarks.

First, there is no doubt a bias against theology in the minds of a great many scientists; and for this theology is very mainly responsible. Century after century it did its best to discourage scientific pursuits; and when it failed in this despicable purpose, it avenged itself by the most cruel, not to say fiendish, persecutions. If you think of Copernicus, Galileo, Bruno; if you read the long, ghastly story of the treatment which for ages scientists received at the hands of theologians; if you remember that many of the opinions which were once defended by torture and by murder, are now known to be absurdly erroneous,—you will understand why those who devote their lives to the pursuit of physical science, should have conceived a dislike for everything that has ever been connected with theology, not excluding even the ideas of the soul and of God, —ideas which theology has so grossly caricatured and abused.

But, secondly, exclusive attention to any pursuit has a tendency to narrow a man's sympathies, and make him intellectually incapable of dealing with matters outside his accustomed sphere of thought. Bacon said, "A little natural philosophy, and the first entrance into it, doth dispose the opinion to atheism; but much natural philosophy, and wading deep into it, will bring about men's minds to religion." Now, judging by the modern scientists, this is not true. Men like Tyndall and Huxley are no tyros in natural philosophy; they have "waded deep into it"; and yet their minds are not brought about to religion. One cause of this, I think, may be found in the fact of their exclusive, or almost exclusive, devotion to physical studies. Men who spend their entire lives in investigating the properties of matter, are very apt to forget that there is anything else, and at last they may become absolutely incapable of conceiving the possibility of immaterial existence.

Scientists seem in the present day to be intoxicated, so to speak, by the magnificence of their triumphs in the study of matter. And at this we can hardly be surprised. Their spectroscopes have revealed the constituent elements of sun and stars. Their geological surveys have shown, written clearly on the rocks, the history of life from the eozoon up to man. Their telescopes have detected, in the Milky Way, planets in the very process of creation. Their microscopes have brought the invisible within the range of vision. They have gone abroad throughout the physical universe, weighing, measuring, analysing, foretelling; and they begin to feel as if nothing could be hid from their instruments of research. "I have swept the heavens with my telescope," said Lalande, "and have not found a God." "We have examined the brain with our miscroscopes," say the physiologists, "and have not found a soul." "The progress of science in all ages," says Professor Huxley, "has meant the extension of the province of what we call matter and causation, and the concomitant gradual banishment, from all regions of human thought, of what we call spirit and spontaneity."

So much the worse for science! There *is* such a thing as spirit, for this is merely a synonym for soul; and, as we have seen, the existence of the soul can be demonstrated. There *is* such a thing as spontaneity, for this is merely a synonym for our power of self-adjustment and our power of adjusting the environment, which Huxley himself allows that we possess. If the progress of science has meant—and I am afraid it has—the banishment from our thoughts of spirit and spontaneity, it has meant the ignoring of certain very important *facts*. And since the business of science is to recognise facts, to ignore them is unscientific. I tell you, whoever denies or ignores the existence of the soul, proves conclusively by so doing that his culture, however great, is one-sided and incomplete; that there has been something unscientific even about his scientific training.

Now, please, understand me. Nothing could be further from my intention, than to speak of the great masters in physical science without becoming respect. I have the highest possible admiration for them. *In there own sphere* they well deserve the title of exact thinkers. I only wish that we, in ours, were always able to imitate their splendid example. I know of nothing nobler, for example, than the conduct of Professor Tyndall in regard to the theory of spontaneous generation. He himself hoped that it would turn out true; and yet, it was by his own laborious efforts that the experiments, previously supposed to have established it, were proved unsatisfactory.

But with all respect to the physicists, what I would most earnestly insist upon is this,—the greatness of their achievements in physics, does not give any authority whatsoever to their views upon other subjects. No one can be an expert in everything. To adopt the opinion of Professor Huxley on questions relating to the soul, is like going to consult the senior wrangler when out of health, or seeking the advice of a bookworm in the purchase of a horse. The wrangler may have amused himself at odd moments by dabbling a little in medicine; the bookworm may have bestridden a horse or two in his day; still we might be excused for feeling a little hesitation in accepting their judgment as infallible. Similarly, the physicist has a mission in the world which cannot be fulfilled by the metaphysical philosopher; and the metaphysical philosopher has a mission which cannot be fulfilled by the physicist. This was once recognised by Professor Tyndall. In the eloquent conclusion to the Belfast address, he says: "The world embraces not only a Newton but a Shakespeare, not only a Boyle but a Raphael, not only a Kant but a Beethoven, not only a Darwin but a Carlyle. Not in each of these, but in all, is human nature whole. They are not opposed, but supplementary; not mutually exclusive, but reconcilable." That is true, though the agnostics, Tyndall himself among the number, are constantly forgetting it. They seem to imagine that human nature will be explained, so far as explanation is possible, by physical investigators alone. But there are other experts, in other departments of human experience, and on what ground can we refuse to listen to them? Ignoring the arguments of the mental philosopher is as one-sided and unjustifiable, as closing one's ears against the teachings of the physical scientist. Finely has Walt Whitman said,— "We will joyfully accept modern science, and loyally follow it; but there remains a still higher flight, a higher fact,—the eternal soul of man. . . . To me the crown of scientism will be, to open the way for a more splendid theology, for ampler and diviner songs."

The ampler songs of which Whitman speaks may not come in your day or mine. Our race as yet is in its babyhood. The agnostics are not alone in their one-sidedness. All men are one-sided more or less. Our vision is blurred, our aims are petty, our sympathies are contracted. But it need not always be so. It will not always be so. There come to some of us now and again moments of prophetic inspiration, when the things of the present are as though they were not, when we live in the far-off future. In a moment such as that I hear an anthem of surpassing, indescribable beauty; and I can distinguish the voices of scientists, as they mingle harmoniously with the voices of poets, philosophers, and saints. The anthem ascends to the eternal throne. It is the offering of perfected humanity to God!

Agnosticism.

III.

THE SOUL'S KNOWLEDGE OF ITSELF.

AGNOSTICISM, which denies the possibility of a knowledge of God, rests, as I have already explained to you, upon the fundamental assumption that we can never know anything but phenomena—that cognisance is restricted, by the very constitution of our minds, to transitory sensations and thoughts. If it were so restricted, knowledge of the soul would be just as impossible as the knowledge of God. That it is not so restricted, appears from the fact that the existence of the soul is demonstrable. When we carefully examine our conscious experience, it is found to involve something which, as it remains identical, must be distinguished from sensations and thoughts that change and pass away. In other words, our conscious experience implies and necessitates a soul. Now the recognition of this soul is the recognition of something that is not phenomenal; and therefore the fundamental assumption of agnosticism is false.

Let us now pass on, from the consideration of the existence of the soul, to discuss the question as to the soul's knowledge of itself. And let us begin by examining the doctrine of Herbert Spencer. In regard to our supposed ignorance of the soul, he takes a somewhat different view from most of the agnostics. Instead of maintaining that there is no reason why we should believe in a soul, he maintains, on the contrary, that the laws of thought compel us to believe in it. But though we are obliged to *believe* in it, we can never according to Herbert Spencer *know* it.

First let us see what he says to show that we are bound to believe in it. "How can consciousness be wholly resolved into impressions and ideas—that is, into sensations and thoughts —when an impression necessarily implies something impressed? Or again, how can the sceptic, who has decomposed his consciousness into impressions and ideas, explain the fact that he considers them as *his?* Or once more, if he admits (as he must) that he has an impression of his personal existence, what warrant can he show for rejecting this impression as unreal, while he accepts all his other impressions as real? Unless he can give satisfactory answers to these questions, which he cannot, he must abandon his conclusions, and must admit the reality of the individual mind."

But having thus shown that we must believe in the soul, he proceeds to argue that we can never know it. "Unavoidable as is this belief [in the existence of the individual soul], established though it is not only by the assent of mankind at large, endorsed by diverse philosophers and by the suicide of the sceptical argument, it is yet a belief admitting of no justification by reason; nay, it is a belief which reason, when pressed for a distinct answer, rejects. The fundamental condition of all consciousness is the antithesis of subject and object." [I had better here, perhaps, stop to explain, for the sake of those who are not accustomed to philosophical terminology, that the word subject stands for the mind which perceives a thing, and the word object for the thing which is perceived. For example, when I look at this book, my mind which apprehends it is the subject, and the book itself is the object. Similarly, if I think of some abstract quality, as for instance of justice, my mind is the subject as before, and the idea or thought of justice is the object. In all consciousness, in all knowledge—as Spencer says—there must necessarily be this union of subject and object.] "But," he continues, "what is the corollary of this doctrine, as bearing on the consciousness of self? The mental act in which self is known implies, like every other mental act, a perceiving subject and an object perceived. If, then, the object perceived is self, what is the subject that perceives? Or if it be the true self which thinks, what other self can be thought of? Clearly the true cognisance of self implies a state, in which the knowing and the known are one, in which subject and object are identified; and this is the annihilation of both. So that the personality of which each is conscious, and of which the existence is to each a fact beyond all others most certain, is yet a thing which cannot be known at all; knowledge of it is forbidden by the very nature of thought."

There is a certain law of thought then, according to Herbert Spencer, which prevents us from knowing ourselves. Now this law, let me ask you carefully to notice, he virtually gives us in the passage I have already quoted, under two different forms. First, thus: all knowledge involves the relation of subject and object. Second, thus: the object must always be something different from the subject.

Now these two modes of statement are not, as he imagines, different ways of expressing the same law; they are totally different laws. The one is a law of nature, the other is only a law of his own. To say that knowledge involves the relation of subject and object, is merely to say that the term knowledge, just like the term sensation, is a single word standing for a double fact, and means something known by some one. There can be no knowledge where there is no one to know; and contrariwise, no one can know, and at the same time know nothing. This is of course a self-evident truth, involved in the very nature of thought. But to say that the object must always be something different from the subject, in other words that the subject can never become an object to itself, is to make a totally different assertion,—an assertion which, so far from being self-evidently true, is evidently, if not self-evidently, false. It is false because, Spencer himself being witness it is contradicted by experience.

I daresay you have heard a story which is told at the expense of the philosopher Zeno. He was one day lecturing to his class on the impossibility of motion, when the students, becoming rather weary, and seeing as they thought a good opportunity for practically refuting their master, got up and walked out, leaving him to finish his lecture to deserted benches. If he had really meant what they thought he meant, this reply would no doubt have been conclusive. Now there is a method of answering objections, to which this story has given a technical name, The method is called *solvitur ambulando:* the objection is answered, the problem is solved, *by walking*—that is, by doing what is alleged to be impossible.

This method may be applied to Herbert Spencer's argument. He says we cannot know ourselves. I reply that, even on his own showing, we do. "Personality," he says, is "a fact of which each one is conscious." Now since consciousness is merely another name for knowledge, and personality is but another name for self, in saying we are conscious of personality he virtually asserts that we know ourselves. Nor is there any vagueness and indistinctness about this knowledge. Personality, he says again, is "the fact, beyond all others, the most certain." Now the things of which we are most certain are, of course, the things which we may most certainly be said to know. And yet the fact which stands first in the order of certainty, Spencer will not allow to stand even last in the order of knowledge, but declares that in regard to it we are, and must ever remain, completely ignorant. It follows then, you see, from Spencer's so-called law of thought, that we are sure of what is somewhat doubtful, but are not sure of that in regard to which there can be no doubt; we may be said to know things of which we are comparatively ignorant, but must be declared ignorant of that which emphatically we know; all facts are knowable except the most certain fact of all, and that is altogether unknowable; in a word ignorance is knowledge and knowledge is ignorance. Hence it must be inferred, that Spencer's supposed law of thought is merely an imagination of his own; for the real *bonâ fide* laws of thought never land us in absurdity.[1]

---

[1] Mr Spencer's confused interpretation of the doctrine of relativity, and his curious identification of the soul with "the Absolute," I have discussed in my 'Belief in God,' pp. 44-49.

Perhaps a parody of Spencer's reasoning may make its fallaciousness more evident. Just as he tries to show the impossibility of self-knowledge, let us try to show the impossibility of self-love. We might say—" The fundamental condition of all love is the antithesis of subject and object. If then the object loved be self, what is the subject that loves? or if it be the true self that loves, what other self can it be that is loved? Self-love implies the identity of subject and object; but, by hypothesis, they must always be different: therefore no man can love himself." Now since in point of fact most persons *do* love themselves, there is manifestly something wrong about this argument. The flaw lies in the hypothesis. It is an arbitrary and false assumption that the object must always be different from the subject. The fallacy is a case of *petitio principii*—the assumption containing by implication the point to be proved. It may be objected that a man does not love himself exactly in the same way as he loves another. But this is no argument for restricting the word " love " to the latter case. On the contrary, since the chief difference often lies in the certainty and intensity of self-love, and the feebleness or doubtfulness of love for others, it might be urged, and indeed has been by Rochefoucauld and others, that men never really love except when they love themselves. The doctrine of Rouchefoucauld may be open to grave question, and I, for one, do not believe it to be true. But if his view were really confirmed by experience, if men's love for others were found to be universally feeble in comparison with their love for themselves, it would follow, when we used the term in its fullest and strictest sense, we should have to say that men loved themselves alone. And so, if personality be, as Spencer says, "a fact above all others the most certain," and if we are going to be very strict in our use of the word knowledge — so strict as to apply it only to that which is pre-eminently worthy of the name — we must say that men never know anything but themselves.

Of course there is a sense in which it may be truly said that we know nothing; for all things affect, and are in turn affected by, all. Since then we do not know everything, we cannot completely know anything. But there is a curious tendency in the present day to overestimate our knowledge of matter, and to underestimate our knowledge of mind. Some one wrote the other day, I observed, to the editor of 'Knowledge,' asking him for an answer to the question, "What is the soul?" The editor replied, "No soul can say." Now, supposing he had been asked, What is a rose or a pebble? I do not know what he would have said; but the same answer would have been no less applicable.

For consider. The physicists differ among themselves as to what matter really is. They are not agreed as to whether it is hard or soft; extended or unextended; altogether antithetical to mind, or in the last resort altogether mental. The resistance which matter offers to pressure was formerly supposed to be produced by the hardness of its particles. But Sir William Thomson, on the contrary, thinks it probable that this resistance is merely the result of a very rapid motion in something that is infinitely soft and yielding. It used to be thought that the ultimate atoms of matter were small, impenetrable bodies, possessing a certain size,—that is, occupying a certain amount of space. But Boscovitch and others have deemed it more likely that these atoms have no size whatever— that they are unextended centres or points of force, through which other forces may penetrate indefinitely. Generally speaking, again, matter is supposed to be the very antithesis and negation of mind. But the late Professor Clifford endeavoured to prove that every molecule of matter in the universe possessed "a small piece of mind-stuff," and that consciousness was merely the result of certain complicated combinations of these elementary molecules. And the eminent evolutionist Mr Wallace suggested, in his 'Contributions to Natural Selection,' that material forces might be the direct outcome of the Divine Will—might be, indeed, that Will itself in action. This disagreement among the physicists proves, of course, that there is no scientific certainty about the ultimate nature of matter.

And what is true of matter in general, is true of any given material object in particular. However much we may know about it, behind our knowledge there lies a background of ignorance. I have often quoted before, and I daresay I shall often quote again, a verse of Tennyson's, which is an exquisite embodiment of a profound metaphysical truth:—

> "Flower in the crannied wall,
> I pluck you out of the crannies,
> Hold you there, root and all, in my hand,
> Little flower; but if I could understand
> What you are, root and all, and all in all,
> I should know what God and man is."

All that we know about the flower is, that it possesses certain qualities—such as size, weight, colour, odour, a particular arrangement of leaves, and so forth. But qualities must be the qualities of something. Or, as this mode of statement would be objected to by the Positivists, who think that qualities may be the qualities of nothing—let me put it thus. There must be something which brings the separate qualities into the unity of an organism, something which makes and keeps the combination of qualities, which we call a flower, different from the combination which we call a weed. This something has never been seen, and cannot even be imagined. Yet flowers and weeds are not therefore declared to be unknowable. We are actually said to have a science,—not knowledge merely, but science, which is classified, systematised knowledge,—we are said to have a science of botany, although there is something in every meanest weed of which we are, and may be for ever, ignorant. By common consent, then, we are considered to know things, when in point of fact we only know their qualities.

Now, in regard to the problem of knowledge, the faculties of the soul correspond exactly to the qualities of material objects. Just as the word flower means the something which combines certain qualities into the unity of a single organism, so the word soul means the something which unites certain faculties into a single personality. It is absurd then to assert, as is sometimes done, that we are necessarily ignorant of the soul, because we can never know anything but its faculties. To know it by its faculties is to know it in a manner precisely similar to that in which the objects of the material world are known.

And, as a matter of fact, it is not true that we only know the soul by its faculties. It is in this way we know the souls of others. Their words and deeds are the evidence of faculties, working together more or less harmoniously, and involving therefore some bond of union, such as is expressed by the word personality. It is by a process of inference that we know the souls of our neighbours. But each of us has a soul of his own; and here our knowledge is intuitive and direct. Our soul is given us in consciousness, as part of that consciousness itself. And it is for this reason that the soul is so pre-eminently, so emphatically knowable. In regard to the objects of the material world, the underlying something, which makes them to be what they are, can only be surmised and guessed at. But along with our mental experience, there is *given* us the underlying something which makes that experience possible, and gathers it up into the unity of a personal life. Consciousness is neither more nor less than the recognised union of the noumenal with the phenomenal. In sensation, I am aware not only that there is something being felt, but that it is I who feel it. In thought, I perceive not only that there is something being thought, but that it is I who think it. In volition, I apprehend not only that there is something being willed, but that it is I who will it. In remembrance, I know not only that certain facts have actually happened, but that I myself have been personally related to them. And of the two elements in consciousness, the personal element is not less certain, but infinitely more certain, than the impersonal. I may be mistaken about sensations; for example, I may fancy I see blue, when in reality what I see is green. I may be mistaken about thoughts; I may fancy I am thinking of holiness, when I am only thinking of narrow-mindedness. I may be mistaken about volitions; I may imagine I am determining to give myself pleasure, when, if I only knew it, I am really determining to give myself pain. My recollection too may sometimes play me false, and my seeming remembrance of events may not be altogether correct. But so far as the personal element in consciousness is concerned, there is no possibility of confusion. I never mistake my own soul for any one else's, nor any one else's soul for my own. Of course I cannot picture my soul in imagination. It would not be a soul if I could: it is only material qualities that are picturable. Of course I cannot define my soul. For to define a thing is to explain it, in terms of something that is better known than itself; but there is nothing which I know better than the soul. The objects of the material world are not always with me to be investigated. My knowledge of them is derived from a merely occasional acquaintance. Even my own body is inconstant, and hands me over every few years to the companionship of another. My soul alone is always with me, given in consciousness along with the feelings and thoughts of which it is the necessary condition, and recognised as remaining persistently itself while they are for ever changing and passing away. So far from being unknowable, the soul is the most knowable existence which the universe contains.

Agnosticism.

IV.

IMMORTALITY.

I WISH to speak to you to-day about the immortality of the soul. In entering on this task I am reminded of a story told by Emerson. Two members of the United States Senate were in the habit of finding, in the midst of their political engagements, as many opportunities as possible for discussing together speculative subjects. Their favourite topic was the immortality of the soul. But they could never discover any satisfactory grounds for believing in it. At last one of them retired from Congress, and went to live in a distant place. They did not meet again till twenty-five years afterwards, and then it was in a crowded reception at the President's house. They had some difficulty in making their way to one another through the brilliant company. When they met, they shook hands long and cordially, but for some time did not utter a word. At last one of them said, "Any light, Albert?" "None," he replied. After a pause the other inquired, "Any light, Lewis?" and the answer again was "None." They looked silently into each other's eyes, gave one more grasp each to the hand he held, and then parted for the last time.

The solemn problem, over which the two senators had puzzled so many years in vain, has been grappled with by the greatest minds of every age; but no one has ever given a completely satisfactory solution. It seems to me that, as yet, the subject has never even been looked at from the best point of view. A favourite argument for immortality used to be derived from the immateriality of the soul. But since matter, so far as we know, is indestructible, the soul's unlikeness to matter, if it proved anything in this connection, would prove its destructibility. The fact is, however, neither materiality nor immateriality has anything to do with duration. Again, the argument from the fact that happiness and perfection are unattainable on earth, only appeals to us if we already believe in a beneficent Creator, who will sooner or later gratify our desires. Similarly the argument that, apart from immortality, God would be unjust, has no force except with those who are firmly persuaded of His justice. But I think, if we follow the line of thought which we have been pursuing for the last three Sundays, the belief in immortality will be found to rest upon much more unassailable ground. The best proof of a future life is to be derived from a careful analysis of our present consciousness.

We have seen that the soul is not only a different existence from the sensation which it feels, but a different kind of existence. The one is transitory; the other is permanent. The sensation passes away; the soul remains persistently behind. This is proved by memory, beyond the possibility of denial. Every time I am engaged in an act of remembrance, I am conscious that it is not a new self, just come into existence, which is so engaged, but the self previously occupied in the manner of which the remembrance is an image. In the complex process of recollection, I am as certain of the persistent identity of the one factor, as I am of the actual existence of the other. The identification of the soul, then, with its own sensations, is the result of an incorrect analysis of consciousness. It comes not of exact, but of inexact, thinking.

The whole of the materialists, and many of the agnostics, fall into a mistake which is even more inexcusable. They actually identify sensations with the physical processes in the brain that precede or accompany them. But there are really no two things in the universe more distinct than a sensation and a neural process. That they are different is proved by my perceiving the one and not perceiving the other. If neural processes were sensations, we should feel them. But we never do, unless through disease something has gone wrong with them; and then we feel, not the sensations to which the neural processes ought to have given rise, but totally different sensations, which should never have come into consciousness at all. And not only is the sensation different from a molecular change in the substance of the brain, but it belongs to a different order of existences—so much so that, though we believe the two things to be connected, we are totally unable to conceive how they can be. This is admitted by Professor Tyndall. In his address to the Physical Section of the British Association in 1868, Tyndall said: "The passage from the physics of the brain to the corresponding facts of consciousness is unthinkable. Granted that a definite thought and a definite molecular action occur in the brain simultaneously, we do not possess the intellectual organ, nor apparently any rudiment of the organ, which would enable us to pass by a process of reasoning from the one phenomenon to the other. They appear together, but we do not know why. Were our minds and senses so expanded, strengthened, and illuminated, as to enable us to see and feel the very molecules of the brain; were we capable of following all their motions, all their groupings, all their electric discharges, if such there be; and were we intimately acquainted with the corresponding states of thought and feeling,—we should be as far as ever from the solution of the problem—How are these physical processes connected with the facts of consciousness? The chasm between the two classes of phenomena would still remain intellectually impassable." Now manifestly two things cannot possibly be identical, when there is an impassable chasm between them. But this distinction, which Tyndall recognised so clearly, the agnostics very frequently altogether fail to perceive.

Once more, the physical organs of perception are often confused with the mental faculties. It is sometimes imagined that sights and sounds are fully explained by a description of the eye and the ear. But an organ of sense is merely, as the word itself signifies, an instrument—an instrument through which the soul receives impressions. As Aristotle and Plato explained long ago, it is not our eyes which see, nor our ears which hear; it is we who see and hear by means of them. If you take away a man's eye, you deprive him of a certain kind of vision, just as you would do by taking away his magnifying-glass. But there is no reason why there should not be other instruments of vision in the universe, as superior to the eye as an astronomer's telescope is superior to a child's. The possibility of perceiving with different organs of perception is faintly illustrated, perhaps, by the proverbial readiness with which, when one of our senses is lost, its place is supplied by others. Blindness, as every one knows, is to some extent atoned for, by the increased acuteness of hearing and of touch.[1] And what is true of one sense is true of all. " It is not even probable that the mind has any kind of relation

---

[1] Compare also the alleged hypnotic power of reading through the forehead.

to the body, which it might not have to any other foreign matter formed into instruments of perception." In point of fact, since the body is constantly changing, we know by experience that the soul *is* related successively to different instruments of perception. The body, then, being merely a mechanical contrivance, through which the soul receives its experiences and performs its work—to confuse the body with the soul is like mistaking a fishing-net for a fisherman, or supposing that a hammer and anvil will constitute a blacksmith!

More frequently however the soul, instead of being identified with the entire body, is identified with the brain. But that my brain is not myself may be proved to demonstration in two ways. First, if I were my brain and my brain were I, in being conscious of myself I should be conscious of my brain; and, with the continual change in its component particles, I should be aware of a corresponding change in my own identity. I should feel that I was being constantly converted into some one else. But I am not conscious of any change in my brain. I am not conscious of my brain at all. I should not know I had a brain unless the physiologists had kindly informed me of the fact. Secondly, the brain is composed of particles, each of which is unconscious. But a number of atoms, unconscious of their diversity, cannot conceivably be combined into a single being conscious of its unity.[1] If anybody thinks they can, he is capable of arguing that a hundred idiots may be worked up into one wise man, or that the President of the Royal Academy is a mere evolution from a paint-pot!

There is then no reason, in the nature of things, why the soul should be destroyed by death. If I were merely a collection of material particles, the breaking-up of the collection would be the annihilation of me. If I were merely a collection of sensations and thoughts, the destruction of the organism on which they depend, would practically amount to my own destruction. But I am a different existence, a different kind of existence altogether, both from my body on the one hand and from my experiences on the other; and therefore my extinction would not necessarily follow either the dissolution of the body, or the cessation of those experiences for which the body is the vehicle. Should my soul at death cease to be, this would not be a case of cause and effect; it would be *a pure coincidence.*

[1] See 'Belief in God,' p. 29.

So far, you will observe, I have spoken as though we were the mere passive recipients of impressions and ideas. But if there is such a thing as *will*, the belief in immortality can be placed on a foundation that is even yet more secure. Let us carry our analysis of consciousness one step further, and inquire into the nature of what is called volition.

Now in order to avoid ambiguity, let us discard the misleading expression free will. It is tautological and absurd. Will must be free, for it means the power of choice, and choice cannot be necessitated. We cannot be compelled to choose one thing, while at the same time we are free to choose either of two things. The question then is not, whether our will is free, but whether we have a will at all.

Of course it is said we have not, by those who deny the existence of the soul. And naturally, for if there is no soul, there is nothing to be free, nothing which can have a will. The brain has no power of choice, nor have sensations and thoughts, either individually or collectively. And it is quite conceivable, of course, that the soul might exist, and be capable of receiving impressions and ideas, and yet be incapable of any spontaneous action of its own. We can imagine, for example, a watch that is conscious but not free. Suppose there is in it a sentient principle which could hear the ticking, and observe the motion of the wheels, and desire a regular kind of existence. It might be able to perceive dust accumulating in its interior, and it might remember, from its past experience, the periodical cleanings which the dust rendered necessary. Such a watch might know, and even foreknow, a good deal about its own condition, but it could in no respect alter it. Whether it went faster or slower, got dirty sooner or later, was cleaned often or seldom, might be to it matters of interest or anxiety; but that would be all. It could not take itself to be cleaned, and it could not in any way modify its circumstances or surroundings. Is this a picture of your life and mine? If so, we are not free.

Most of you will say that this is a gross caricature of human life, and that consciousness informs you unmistakably as to the fact of your freedom. But then the agnostics will tell you, in reply, that you have misunderstood and misinterpreted your consciousness. Your fancied freedom, they assert, is a fancy only. In such matters as these the agnostics do not take much trouble about proof. They have a curious way of assuming that their own opinion must be right, and that they themselves are the only authoritative interpreters of consciousness.

Very well, suppose they are. We can argue the matter from premises which the agnostics have supplied. I will stake the whole question of human freedom upon two sentences of Professor Huxley's; in fact, one of them would be sufficient for my purpose. His general opinion is—as, of course, you know—that we are not free agents; that we are mere machines worked by vital forces. And yet he says, without seeing the inconsistency, "A human being, though a machine, is capable, within certain limits, of self-adjustment." And again: "Our volition counts for something, as a condition of the course of events." That a man of his enormous ability should not see the inconsistency, is a striking illustration of the helplessness — the almost childish helplessness—of the physicists, when they wander from their proper sphere of thought. Since a machine is incapable of self-adjustment,[1] to say that I am capable of it,

---

[1] I need scarcely say that the so-called self-adjusting machines work, like all other machines, in accordance with the intention of the maker, and not in accordance with their own.

is to say that I am not a machine. Since the desire of a being under absolute restraint does not count for anything as a condition of the course of events, to say that mine does, is to say that I am so far free. I may take it then, Professor Huxley being witness, that I have a will.

Let us proceed to inquire what is will? The characteristic of a volition is this—you do not receive it, you make it. It does not come to you, it proceeds from you. It does not arise spontaneously, like sensations or thoughts or desires; but, on the contrary, you create it. For example, under circumstances of provocation a desire may spring up in your mind to revenge yourself by a spiteful remark. But you may determine to pause and to reflect; finally, you may think better of it and hold your tongue. The tendency of the desire was at once to hurry you into speaking bitterly; and had you been merely a conscious machine—an object capable of receiving desires, but incapable of resisting them—you would have yielded to the impulse of passion. But by a sheer effort of will you arrested the desire in its impetuous progress; you refused to be driven by it; you checked, curbed, crushed it. The soul therefore, by its faculty of volition, regulates the expenditure of energy in the tissues of the body, so that it may survive, not only the physical organism, but the entire physical universe.

If the soul were one of the energies of nature it would expend itself in doing work, it would so to speak be constantly running down, getting changed into less available forms. According to the law of Conservation energy always remains constant in quantity, but according to the law of Dissipation it is always passing into a lower quality. In the history of the physical universe there must come a period of equally diffused heat, when no more transformation will be possible, and therefore no more life or development or change of any kind whatsoever. But the soul, the director of energy, does not come under the sway of this universal law.[1]

[1] One of my reviewers says that this argument, though valid as regards the survival of "an integral part of the soul," viz., will, has nothing to do with personal immortality. I had better perhaps explain, therefore, that the will is not an integral part of the soul, but the soul itself in action. The mind's faculties are not so many parts of itself, but so many ways in which it exercises or manifests itself. The continued existence of the soul's power of choice—since we cannot imagine 0 or *nothing* choosing—implies and necessitates the continued existence of the soul itself. Any argument, therefore, in favour

Well then it is proved, if not that we shall be immortal, at any rate that, according to the ascertained laws of nature, we ought to be. I believe that after what is called my death, my soul will continue to exist, for the same reason which leads me to expect that the sun will continue to rise. While nature remains uniform, death will no more put out the soul than it will put out the sun. All the talk, of which we hear so much in the present day, about there being no soul, or no soul but brain, or no soul that is likely to survive the death of the body—all this is pure nonsense, illogical and unscientific to the last degree. It is certain, demonstrable beyond the possibility of doubt—(1) that we have a soul; (2) that the soul remains persistently identical, while its body and experiences change; (3) that there is no reason why death should put an end to the soul; (4) that, on the contrary, there is the strongest reason—namely, the uniformity of nature—why it should not. The lessons of our childhood then, though mingled no doubt with error, had a firm foundation in fact. And Wordsworth's Ode to Immortality, which is per-

---

of the immortality of the will, can be neither more nor less than an argument in favour of the immortality of the soul, *i.e.*, of personal immortality.

haps the most spiritual poem in any language, is no creation of a diseased brain; it is the outcome of a strictly " scientific use of the imagination ":—

> " The soul that rises with us—our life's star—
>   Hath had elsewhere its setting,
>   And cometh from afar,
>   .   .   .   .   .
>   Hence in a season of calm weather,
>   Though inland far we be,
>   Our souls have sight of that immortal sea
>   Which brought us hither;
>   Can in a moment travel thither;
>   And see the children sport upon the shore,
>   And hear the mighty waters rolling evermore."

Agnosticism.

V.

EVOLUTION OF SPECIES.

LET us take a brief survey of the ground over which we have already travelled. The fundamental principle of agnosticism is, that knowledge is necessarily restricted to what are technically called phenomena—that is, to those things which are capable of being apprehended by the senses. What cannot become a sensation must, the agnostics tell us, for ever remain unknown. Now we saw that this general principle of theirs was false; for the soul, though it can never be apprehended by the senses, is knowable and known. The existence of a soul is a necessary condition for the existence of sensations. The very meaning of the word sensation is something felt by some one—that is to say, by a soul.

Further, when we investigated the faculty of memory, we discovered that the soul was distinguished from transitory and changing phenomena by its permanence and identity. The very meaning of the word remembrance is, that one and the self-same soul has existed in two different states—viz., in its present state of recollection, and also in the previous state of which this recollection is a copy. The soul, having thus existed in successive states, must beyond question have persisted between them. We saw that there was no reason to suppose this persistence would cease with death; but that, on the contrary, there was every reason to suppose it would not. Waiving however the question of the soul's persistence in another life, we took our stand upon the undeniable fact of its persistence in this, and we saw that its persistent and non-phenomenal character, so far from making it unknowable, rendered it on the contrary pre-eminently knowable. There is nothing in the universe we know so well, for the simple reason that it is present and identical in all our experiences, while those experiences themselves are for ever changing and passing away. The only plausible reasons for supposing the soul to be unknown are—(1) that we cannot picture it; and (2) that we cannot define it. The answer to the first objection is this: only what is material is picturable; the soul being immaterial, is therefore necessarily unpicturable; anything that could be pictured would not be a soul. And as regards the second objection—viz., its undefinableness—the answer is, that we can only define a thing by referring it to something better known than itself. The soul therefore is, from the very nature of the case, undefinable, because it is itself the best known.

Now let us pass on, from the knowledge of the soul, to the knowledge of God. If the agnostics had been right in asserting that only phenomena could be known, it would follow necessarily that God, if a God there were, not being a phenomenon, must from His very nature be unknowable. But, conversely, as the soul is knowable, it follows that knowledge is not restricted to phenomena; and hence, for anything our experience tells us to the contrary, God *may be* known. We have thus got rid of an objection that barred the way to all further inquiry. The demonstration of the knowableness of the soul is a demonstration that all knowledge is not phenomenal. In other words, there is nothing in the nature of things, or in the constitution of our faculties, which would render the knowledge of God an *a priori* impossibility. Let us now proceed to inquire into its actuality. Having discovered that we may know God, let us ask, Do we in reality know Him?

The agnostics, though not dogmatically denying the existence of God, very frequently maintain that our experience—so far as it goes—seems to imply His non-existence, or at any rate His utter separation from the present system of things. Theologians have always attempted to explain nature by the hypothesis of design or purpose. They have maintained that the order, harmony, and adaptation which we see around us, necessarily involve the existence of a Being, personal, conscious, and intelligent, by whose volition this order and adaptation have been produced. But now the agnostics will have it, that the theories of evolution and natural selection give a full and sufficient explanation of the universe, without any reference to supernatural design or purpose; and indeed they sometimes go so far as to assert, that these theories are quite incompatible with the supposition, that God has had anything whatever to do with the world in which we find ourselves.

Now I want you to investigate this matter. It is too late in the day to defend religion by asserting that the theories in question are false, for to some extent they are demonstrably and undeniably true. But let us carefully discuss their real bearing upon the existence and knowableness of God. I think we shall discover that, taken by themselves, they do not give a complete and final explanation of natural phenomena; and that, so far from being incompatible with a supernatural purpose, they distinctly imply and necessitate it.

In one sense it must be admitted that design has been for ever disproved. The kind of design which Paley supposed himself to have discovered in nature, is not to be found there. He fancied that every organism, and every part of every organism, had been individually adapted and contrived by the Creator for the accomplishment of a definite end, just as each portion of a watch is the result of a particular act of contrivance, on the part of the man who made it. The God of Paley was merely a great Mechanician—spelt with a capital M, it is true, but employing means and methods for the accomplishment of His purposes, more or less similar to those which would be used by a human workman.

This view, in addition to its *a priori* improbability, has been disproved by facts, especially by those facts with which we have become acquainted in the study of comparative anatomy. We frequently find in animals what are called rudimentary or abortive organs, which are manifestly not adapted to any end, which never can be of any use, and whose presence in the organism is sometimes positively injurious. For example, there are snakes that have small rudimentary legs—so rudimentary that they cannot walk upon them. The cowfish has the rudiments of an arm and hand, highly developed and yet perfectly useless. The bones of this organ exactly correspond to those which are found in a human being: there are the five fingers, with every joint distinct; but they are enclosed in a stiff, inflexible skin, so that not a joint can ever move. Similarly, there are insects that have wings with which they can never fly—wings that are tightly fastened down and enclosed in sheaths. Again, an unborn mole possesses eyes; but though they are perfect in themselves at that early stage of his existence, they dry up before he has the chance of seeing with them. Man himself has aborted organs. In the os coccyx there are from three to five vertebræ of a tail. And what is called the *appendix vermiformis*, corresponds exactly to an organ which is useful enough in birds and marsupials, but in the human body it is not only useless but dangerous. If a hard substance, such as an orange-pip, lodges in it, the result may sometimes be inflammation and death; and in other indirect ways it is not unfrequently a source of mischief. Such facts as these—and the instances might be multiplied indefinitely—are perfectly intelligible on the theory of evolution, but are absolutely inconsistent with Paley's theory of design. It is inconceivable that organs which never do any good, still more that organs which sometimes do a great deal of harm, should have been specially designed and contrived by God.

And further, not only are there *parts* of organisms which we cannot believe to have been individually designed, but we also find in nature *entire* organisms—whole species of animals—so inexpressibly horrible and loathsome, that if they were directly and for their own sakes created by any one, it must have been by a being who preferred hideousness to beauty. Think of creatures like the squid, which you saw a few years ago in the Fisheries Exhibition, or the octopus, whose detestableness has been immortalised by Victor

Hugo in the 'Toilers of the Sea.' Such monsters may have been inevitably produced during the natural course of evolution; but if they came into existence by a special creative fiat, that fiat must have proceeded from a Being in all respects opposite to Him whom we call God.

I will not insist much, however, upon this point, as it may be considered a matter of taste rather than of reason. I take my stand upon the existence of abortive organs, and I say that fact alone is sufficient to prove conclusively, that the method of the Creator is not the method of a human mechanician. No machinist ever hampered or disfigured his machine by utterly useless adjuncts; still less would he purposely put into it anything which was likely to interfere with its successful working, or to lead to its ultimate destruction. The method of creation then, whatever it may be, is certainly not Paley's method. So far as I am aware, no one who is capable of forming an opinion on the subject, no educated person in the present day, any longer believes in Paley's theory. We may regard it as finally and for ever exploded.

The doctrine which has taken its place, which to some extent and to a greater or less degree all intelligent persons have accepted, is the doctrine of evolution—the doctrine, viz., that species have been produced, not by distinct creative acts, but by transmutation and descent from one, or at any rate a comparatively few, primordial types.

It might have been expected that comparative anatomy alone would have been sufficient to establish the theory of evolution; for this theory is the only one which will account for the facts which the study of comparative anatomy has brought to light. The useless rudiments of organs in one species are easily explained by evolution, as having been transmitted from another species to which, in their fully developed and useful forms, they properly belonged. Cuvier, Linnæus and others, however, still held, anatomy notwithstanding, to the old view, that each species of animals had been separately created, and that it was absolutely immutable, altogether incapable of giving rise to a different species, no matter what the pressure of circumstances, no matter what the lapse of time. But since the days of Cuvier, our knowledge has enormously increased, and the evidence that the old view is untenable has become overwhelming.

In the first place, the division of animals into species is an altogether arbitrary division.

Though species were thought to be immutable, varieties were known to be mutable; but between species and varieties it is impossible to draw any definite distinction. "Few well-marked and well-known varieties," says Darwin, "can be named, which have not been ranked as species by at least some competent judges." The difference, therefore, between species and varieties, is only one of degree; and there is nothing in the nature of the former to prevent a transmutation, similar to that which actually takes place in the latter. And since we know, from our experience with domesticated animals, that one variety may be transmuted into another variety, we are compelled to believe that, given the greater length of time demanded by the greater amount of divergence, one species may be similarly transmuted into another species.

And in the second place, this *a priori* possibility, confirmed, as we have seen it to be, by the teaching of anatomy, may now be considered a demonstrated fact, thanks to the additional light which has been thrown upon the subject by geology, palæontology and embryology. These sciences have put the blood-relationship of species beyond a doubt. The embryos of existing animals are found, again and again, to bear the closest resemblance to extinct species, though in the adult form the resemblance is obscured. In some cases we have discovered in geological strata the intermediate links, through which one species has ascended, so to speak, into another. The series of gradations could not have been more palpable, had we actually witnessed the transformation. In the archæopteryx at the British Museum, we see a bird emerging from the reptile state of existence. It has the finger-like claws of a reptile; and it has a reptile's tail, with the addition of some feathers. Similarly in the iguanodon we have an instance of a creature going up, as it were, in the scale of being. It was more a reptile than anything else; yet it walked on its hind legs, and had a snout prolonged like a beak. But of all instances of verified gradation, that afforded by the horse is the most complete and striking. Between our existing species and the orohippus of the Eocene period, four intermediate fossil species have been discovered, making six in all. The first of these, the orohippus, has four toes; next to him comes an equine animal, with three toes and a large splint, as it is called, replacing the aborted fourth toe; then an animal with three toes and a very small splint; then three toes without a splint; then one toe and two splints; and lastly, we have our one-toed horse, in which the two splints of the species that preceded him have almost disappeared. And when we learn that these fossil animals were found in different geological strata, that the one which differs most from our own horse was discovered in the lowest or first deposited stratum, and the one which differs least in the highest or last deposited stratum—in other words, that these six equine species inhabited the earth in the order of time corresponding exactly to the order of gradation—we have no alternative but to conclude that the last is a lineal descendant of the first.

It is impossible, then, for those who have the slightest respect for truth, to ignore the theory of evolution. Its expounders differ, as we shall presently see, in the scope which they ascribe to it; but though there are differences of opinion as to the range of the law, the fact of its being a law, a fundamental law, of nature, is no longer a matter that can be denied or even doubted. The knowableness of God, if it is to be proved at all, must be proved upon the understanding that evolution is the method, or at any rate one of the methods, by which nature works.

Any theologian who denies or ignores this, places himself by so doing beyond the pale of controversy. *Falsum in uno falsum in omnibus.* If you begin to argue from a falsehood, you can only reach a falsehood in the conclusion; or if your conclusion should happen to be true, your reasoning must have been bad, your seeming argument can have no coherence—it is only a piece of nonsense.

Many good persons dislike the doctrine of evolution, because they find it often held in combination with the theories of agnosticism, materialism, or atheism. I shall hope to show you that there is no necessary connection between evolution and any of these disheartening doctrines; and that, on the contrary, the inference from the one to the other is illogical. In the meantime, I would suggest for your consideration the thought, that evolution is mainly, if not entirely, concerned with the superficial changes and developments that we can see and touch. But the dwelling-place of the Almighty is not upon the surface of things. If we are ever to find God, we must look far below the region with which the evolutionist is busied, deep down into that inner nature of things, concerning which our eyes and hands can bring us no report. The work of evolution is discovered by the senses. But the divinest work of God is only to be detected by the mind and the spirit. To see the one and not the other, is to miss the beauty of the fairest half of the universe.

" The works of God are fair for nought,
    Unless our eyes, in seeing,
See hidden in the thing the thought
    That animates its being.

The outward form is not the whole,
    But clearly has been moulded
To image forth an inward soul,
    That dimly is unfolded.

The shadow pictured in the lake
    By every tree that trembles,
Is cast for more than just the sake
    Of that which it resembles.

The dew falls lightly, not alone
    Because the meadows need it,
But hath an errand of its own
    To human souls that heed it.

The stars are lighted in the skies
    Not merely for their shining,
But, like the light of loving eyes,
    Have meanings worth divining.

The waves that moan along the shore,
    The winds that sigh in blowing,
Are sent to teach a mystic lore
    Which men are wise in knowing.

The clouds around the mountain-peak,
    The rivers in their winding,
Have secrets, which to all who seek
    Are precious in the finding.

Thus nature dwells within our reach;
    But though we stand so near her,
We still interpret half her speech
    With ears too dull to hear her.

Whoever at the coarsest sound
    Still listens for the finest,
Shall hear the noisy world go round
    To music the divinest.

Whoever yearns to see aright,
    Because his heart is tender,
Shall catch a glimpse of heavenly light
    In every earthly splendour.

So since the universe began,
    And till it shall be ended,
The soul of nature, soul of man,
    And soul of God are blended."

Agnosticism.

VI.

EVOLUTION OF THE ANIMAL AND VEGETABLE KINGDOMS.

WE are engaged in considering the knowledge of God. Now by God we mean, among other things, the Being from whom this world has come, the Being of whose mind and will nature is the expression. But it is evident that if nature is in any sense connected with God, our knowledge of the two must harmonise. God cannot be what nature plainly declares He is not. And though He may be a great deal more, He must be, at least, what nature plainly declares that He is. The knowledge of nature is thus one of the first steps to the knowledge of God. "That is not first which is spiritual, but that which is natural, and afterward that which is spiritual." Unless we know nature which we have seen, how can we know God whom we have not seen? The Divine Being has, perhaps, other — and what may seem to us higher — methods of working than those which nature suggests. But He certainly does not work by methods which nature plainly contradicts. An investigation of our knowledge of nature, therefore, is an essential preliminary to anything like an adequate discussion of our knowledge of God. What we *can* know of God will depend to some extent upon what we *do* know of nature. I admit that there are other and better ways of knowing Him than through the instrumentality of material phenomena. But the philosophic mind can only be satisfied, when it sees that the information which comes from the superior sources of knowledge, is not out of harmony with that which is imparted by the inferior.

We have seen that there are two competing theories which profess to explain the phenomena of nature—namely, Paley's and Darwin's. According to the first, every animal or vegetable species, every individual organism and every portion of every organism, are supposed to have been directly and specially designed and created by God. But this theory, as I pointed out, was completely disproved by facts, and in particular by the existence of rudimentary and abortive organs, which, so far from answering any definite purpose, are at the best useless, and not unfrequently injurious. But these and other circumstances, with which the first theory are in flagrant contradiction, are completely accounted for by the second. The latter theory is variously termed the theory of evolution, descent, filiation, or transmutation; and is so called because it asserts that all species of animals and all species of plants, which have ever existed or which still exist on the earth, are derived from one, or a few, simple forms. This theory had been brought forward and defended in the beginning of the present century by several eminent naturalists, especially by Lamarck and Goethe; but it received its complete demonstration mainly through the efforts of Darwin, and is therefore called the Darwinian theory. It is now accepted to some extent by all scientific experts.

Next comes the question—In what manner has evolution been effected? What is its immediate physical cause? What is there in the nature of species or their surroundings which leads to their transmutation into other species? Lamarck and the earlier apostles of evolution endeavoured to account for it by supposing an inherent tendency in every organism to self-improvement—an inherent tendency to adapt itself more and more to its environment. The length of a giraffe's neck, according to this theory, would be due to the fact that its ancestors in remote generations had found their own necks inconveniently short, and had therefore made continual, and in time successful, efforts to stretch them. But against this theory of Lamarck's it is urged, among other objections, that even supposing it to exist, there are many modifications, serving to fit organisms to their environment, for which it will not account. For instance, " by no process of direct adjustment," says Herbert Spencer, " could an egg-shell come to have the required thickness. If the shells were too weak, the eggs which a bird laid would be broken or cracked. But these breakages or crackings could not react on the maternal organism, could not lead to the production of thicker shells, unless we suppose that the bird understood the cause of the evil, and was able by its own will to control the thickness of the shell."

The principle which is now supposed to account for all organic development, and which undoubtedly does account for the great majority of them, is the principle of natural selection. It was discovered, as you know, almost simultaneously by Darwin and Mr Wallace. Let me give it you in Darwin's words: "As many more individuals of each species are born than can possibly survive, and as consequently there is a frequently recurring struggle for existence, it follows that any being, if it vary however slightly in a manner profitable to itself under the complex conditions of life, will have a better chance of surviving, and thus be naturally selected. And afterwards, from the strong principle of inheritance, any selected variety will tend to propagate its new and modified form." That is to say, there is an inherent tendency in all species to vary indefinitely from the original type; and any variation which is profitable to its possessor is seized upon by nature and perpetuated. Organic development is thus no longer attributable to an animal's voluntary efforts, but is thought to be the direct work of nature, irrespective of the animal's wishes and will. "The giraffe," says Mr Wallace, "did not lengthen its neck by stretching it; but among its shorter-necked ancestors some would have necks a little longer than the rest, and this enabled them, on the first scarcity of food, to secure a fresh range of pasture, and so to outlive their less fortunate comrades." This theory justifies itself by accounting for a great many facts which Lamarck's supposition failed to cover. For example, to take the case of the egg-shell,—only when the shell was strong enough not to crack, would a bird be produced from it; and this peculiarity, to which the bird would owe her own life, she must, by the laws of heredity, transmit. Strong-shelled eggs would therefore be perpetuated, because only strong-shelled eggs could survive. That this principle of natural selection is at least one of the methods by which evolution has been effected, is no longer doubted by any one whose opinion is worth being discussed.

You see, then, the changed position of the argument from design. We can no longer say that every individual organism, or every distinct species of organism, implies a distinct creative act. On the contrary all the evidence we have tends to the conclusion that species, as they now exist, have been evolved from more or less different species, and that this process of evolution is the result of a very simple natural cause: in the struggle for existence the weakest have died out and the strongest or fittest have survived. The characteristics in which existing animals and vegetables differ from their remote ancestors, are the very characteristics which render them better adapted than those ancestors could have been to the present environment.

Up to this point all competent critics are agreed. Now comes the question, How far will the principle of evolution carry us? I have spoken almost exclusively of the transmutation of animal species; but of course, *mutatis mutandis*, the same remarks will apply to the transmutation of vegetable species. One species of vegetable is evolved from another species of vegetable, in a manner precisely analogous to that in which one species of animal is evolved from another species of animal. And here we are confronted with the question, May both the animal and vegetable kingdoms have had a common origin? or is there an impassable gulf between them? Let us just see how matters stand. Each kingdom may be classified under six great divisions. The animal kingdom is commonly divided into vertebrate animals, articulated (subdivided into the arthropoda and vermes), molluscs, and radiated animals (subdivided into the echinodermata and zoophytes). The vegetable kingdom is commonly divided into flowering plants, ferns, mosses, lichens, fungi, and water-weeds. Now the animals included in each of the six animal tribes, the vegetables included in each of the six vegetable tribes, notwithstanding great variety in external form and internal structure, possess nevertheless such numerous and important characteristics in common, that there can be no doubt of their having sprung from a common ancestry.

It is at this point, I want you specially to notice, that *demonstrated* evolutionism may be said to end. Darwin's assertion was, that all species were descended "from one, or a few, primordial types." It has been proved beyond dispute that they have not come from many. But in passing on to inquire whether *the whole organic world* has had a *single* origin, we are going from the region of fact into that of supposition. Still there are reasons — strong, though not amounting to demonstration — for believing that the six animal tribes are connected at their roots, and that the six vegetable tribes are connected at theirs; in other words, that all animals have developed out of one primordial ancestor, and that all vegetables have done the same. Nay, a further investigation makes it not improbable that the two great kingdoms are themselves ultimately connected.

and that animals and plants have been alike derived from some primary living creature.

The grounds for this supposition are the following. It is impossible to draw any absolute line of demarcation between the animal and vegetable worlds. The higher animals and plants, it is true, are readily distinguished from one another, because the former (the higher animals) possess a nervous system and the power of locomotion, while the latter (the higher plants) do not. But these distinctions do not hold good as regards the lower and less organised members of the two kingdoms. Many animals have no nervous system, and many plants have the power of locomotion. It used to be considered that animals could always be distinguished from plants by the nature of their food. As a general rule they can; for plants are almost always endowed with a power of which animals, generally speaking, are destitute —the power, viz., of converting inorganic matter into organic. The food of plants consists of inorganic compounds, such as carbonic acid, ammonia, and mineral salts. Out of these simple elements they manufacture that very complex substance called protoplasm, which is found without exception in every living organism, and which has therefore been considered "the physical basis of life." But there are certain plants, of the fungi class, which are incapable of manufacturing their own protoplasm, which can only be nourished by compounds that are already organised and already therefore contain protoplasm. So that the last distinction which was supposed to represent an impassable barrier between the animal and vegetable worlds—the distinction of food—may now be considered to have broken down.

And further, since the development of the microscope, there have been discovered an enormous number of objects, called by Haeckel Protista or primary creatures, possessing such a remarkable mixture of animal and vegetable properties, that naturalists have been quite unable to agree as to which kingdom they really belonged. Many of them, as Haeckel amusingly puts it, botanists defined as animals, and zoologists as plants; neither of the two would own them. Others again were declared by botanists to be plants, and by zoologists to be animals; each wanted to claim them. Haeckel himself proposes to comprise these Protista in a third organic kingdom, standing midway between the other two, which he calls the *Regnum pro-*

tisticum. And as they possess the qualities both of animals and vegetables, they would appear to bridge over the gulf that was formerly supposed to be impassable.

There seems nothing then to contradict, but on the other hand a good deal to confirm, the supposition that plants and animals may have had the same origin; that they may both have sprung from one primary source; that in all their multitudinous varieties they may have been evolved from a single living creature. This has not been proved, as Haeckel himself admits; but it may be proved presently; and it is safer for the theologian, I think, to assume that it will be, if he wishes to put theology upon a basis that can never be moved.

Now if, for the sake of argument, we make this assumption, the next question that suggests itself for our consideration is this—Whence came that first living creature, from which the animal and vegetable worlds have been evolved? Does it necessarily demand for its explanation a special creative act? or may life itself be an evolution? Upon this subject, before proceeding further, I must say a few words next week.

But some one says to me—Sir, you have got me to church under false pretences. I came to hear a sermon upon religion, and I have only heard a lecture upon science. Such conduct would be scarcely pardonable in a clergyman during the week, but on Sunday in a pulpit it is sacrilegious." And another critic, less severe but equally shocked, asks me, more in sorrow than in anger, if I really think I am fulfilling my ordination vows—if I really think that I am preaching the Gospel? Yes, my friend, I do. I have never preached anything but the Gospel, and I never shall. What is the Gospel? What is it but the glad tidings that we have a Father in heaven, whom Jesus Christ came to reveal? And what is preaching the Gospel but bringing this truth, in all its many-sidedness, to bear upon modern life? Now the most striking characteristics of our age are, on the one hand the progress of science, and on the other the widespread belief that this progress will result in the destruction of religion. Of course there are many persons who know nothing about the progress of science; and there are others who wilfully blind their eyes to it, as to an unpleasant subject which it is best for them to ignore. But such persons, as one can see at a glance, are scarcely, if at all, represented in the congregation before me; and at any rate it is needless to say that to such persons these sermons are not addressed. Some of you, I know, are experts in science; many of you follow with the keenest interest the course of scientific thought; and most of you, I believe, are honest enough to feel that not even to win heaven itself—were it conceivable that heaven could be so won—would you profess to believe that the truth of science is a lie. But keen as is your interest in science, your interest in religion is keener still. And in these days of rampant agnosticism you sometimes tremble for the Ark of God. It is my object then in this series of sermons—it is my object, for your benefit and for my own, to take a brief but calm survey of the discoveries and theories which are frequently supposed to have destroyed the very possibility of religion; and then, after having looked them boldly in the face, to inquire what is their actual bearing upon our knowledge of God. It is the great problem of the age; and he who says the Gospel has nothing to do with it, virtually asserts that Christianity is an antiquated and worn-out creed—virtually represents Christ, its author, as an object for the scorn, or at any rate the pity, of all educated men.

Agnosticism.

VII.

EVOLUTION OF LIFE.

WE are engaged in considering to what extent, and in what manner, our knowledge of God is affected by the discoveries and theories of modern science. In taking a brief preliminary survey of these discoveries and theories, we have seen it must now be considered proved, that the different species of plants and animals, instead of being separately created, were derived — partly at any rate under the influence of natural selection—from a few primordial forms. And further, we have seen there are reasons—strong, though not perhaps amounting to demonstration—for supposing that the entire animal and vegetable world has been developed from a single primary living object. Now the question arises, Was that first living object a direct creation? or may life itself be an evolution from non-living matter?

Darwin *assumed* that the primordial form, or forms, had been directly called into existence by the Creator. But his followers have not been content to stop here. They have endeavoured to push the doctrine of evolution farther, and to make it account for the origin of life itself. An ingenious theory was started some time ago by Sir William Thomson, to the effect that the germs of life had been brought to our planet upon the meteoric stones, which came from distant parts of space. It is manifest, however, that this theory only postpones the difficulty. Sooner or later we must face the question, Whence came the first life? And before we can answer it, we must inquire whether there is any distinctive difference— and if so, what—between animate and inanimate objects.

Till quite recently it would have been said that they differed unmistakably from each other by the presence, or absence, of organisation. Animate bodies, it would have been said, are always composite in their structure, consisting of dissimilar, heterogeneous parts, which serve as organs or instruments, and work together for the discharge of a variety of functions. On the other hand, the most perfect anorgana—viz., crystals—consist entirely of homogeneous matter, and their structure is not composite but simple. But this distinction has broken down since Haeckel's discovery of monera. You remember I pointed out to you, that the gulf between the animal and vegetable worlds seemed to have been bridged over by the Protista—living creatures that possess the essential characteristics of both worlds. Among these Protista, Haeckel has discovered some objects which he calls monera, and which would seem, in a similar manner, to bridge over the gulf between the organic world and the inorganic. For these monera are, as he says, "organisms without organs." They are without organs, inasmuch as their whole body consists only of a single, perfectly homogeneous lump of protoplasmic slime, in which the strongest microscope can detect no distinction of structure. And yet they are organisms, inasmuch as they go through all the functions of life. They wriggle about in the sprightliest manner. They project and withdraw little filaments like arms and legs. They feed upon atoms which accidentally become imbedded in their surface. And when they have outgrown their normal size, they reproduce themselves by splitting up into two. The possession then of what are properly called organs, would no longer seem to be essential to life.

And not only are we unable to distinguish by *internal organism* the living world from the non-living; we are equally incapable of distinguishing it by its *external form*. The forms of crystals, it is true, are mathematically determinable, limited by plane surfaces which meet in straight lines at certain measurable angles. Vegetable and animal forms, on the contrary, do not, as a rule, admit of such geometrical determination. They are, for the most part, limited by curved surfaces and crooked lines meeting at variable angles. But recently, among the lower organisms, large numbers of living creatures have been discovered, whose forms are bounded, just like those of crystals, by definite, geometrically determined planes and angles. And there are also perfectly amorphous organisms—viz., the monera and amœbæ—which change their forms every moment, and in which we are as little able to point out the definite, fundamental form, as in the case of stones or deposits of mud. We cannot then find any essential difference, either in the external form or in the internal structure, of animate and inanimate bodies.

But it may be said, notwithstanding this fact, that the functions and processes of life are infinitely more mysterious and wonderful than anything which takes place in the inorganic world, and must be attributed to some non-material principle (call it vital force, or what you please) — a principle quite distinct from any of the chemical forces which it takes into its service. But *are* organic phenomena so much more mysterious and wonderful than inorganic? When we compare the growth of a crystal with the growth of a living creature, we find a remarkable similarity between the two processes. If saltpetre is dissolved in boiling water and the water allowed to cool, after a time little bodies, like delicate needles, are observed darting about in all directions, and gradually joining one another in certain definite and regular ways. By dissolving the saltpetre, we have divided it into minute invisible particles. But as the water cools, their mutual attraction draws them together, and they unite, not into mere shapeless lumps, but each little molecule, as it joins the rest, places itself in the proper position to help in building up the beautiful symmetrical rods, which we call saltpetre-crystals. If we repeat the same experiment with a variety of substances, we shall find them assuming different characteristic forms. Gold and copper crystallise in a cubical form, bismuth and antimony hexagonally, iodine and sulphur rhombically. There seems therefore good ground for Haeckel's assertion, that crystallisation is just as mysterious as the development of the most perfect living organism.[1] The growth of the crystal arises from the fact, that new particles continually pass over from the fluid state into the solid, and deposit themselves in certain positions according to certain laws. In like manner, the growth of organisms takes place by the accession of fresh particles. But while the crystals add the new substance externally, organisms absorb it internally; the one grows by addition, the other by intussusception.

The only difference then between the animate and inanimate world, which seems to have survived scientific investigation, is that living bodies *absorb* new matter, and non-living bodies only *add* it to their surface. It remains to inquire, what is the cause of this difference?

At first we should be inclined to think it

[1] Cf. Ruskin's 'Ethics of the Dust.'

was due to the different nature of the materials, of which the animate and inanimate bodies are composed. And there is a substance—namely, protoplasm — which is universally absent from the latter, and universally present in the former. "From the green scum in a stagnant pool up to the most perfect animal organism, and through all the variety of animated beings which lie between them, wherever there is life there is protoplasm." But on further investigation this protoplasm, which is the invariable concomitant or basis of life, is found to be nothing more than a combination of certain *inorganic* elements, such as carbon, nitrogen, phosphorus, and iron. Since then living bodies cannot be distinguished from non-living bodies by the *elements* of which they are composed, it follows that the difference must lie in the character of the composition itself—that is to say, in the manner in which these elements have been combined. In what then, let us ask, does protoplasm differ from other compounds? It differs in two ways: (1) it is very complex; and (2) it is semi-fluid. All inorganic, non-living compounds are comparatively simple substances; but protoplasm is highly complicated, containing many elements united together in definite, but peculiar, proportions. And again, all inorganic, non-living compounds exist either in a solid, fluid, or gaseous state; and these states, as they depend upon, and can be altered by, temperature, may be considered three phases of one and the same state. Protoplasm exists in a fourth condition; it is semi-fluid. It is neither solid like stone, nor liquid like water, but in a medium condition; its particles are in a soft state of aggregation.

The difference in the state of aggregation will account, Haeckel thinks, for the different method of growth followed by an organism on the one hand, and by a crystal on the other. The semi-fluid condition of protoplasm enables the organism which contains it to *absorb* new particles; whereas the crystals, which are destitute of protoplasm, can only take on the particles *externally*. Haeckel further supposes that the semi-fluid state of density peculiar to protoplasm, may be ultimately traced to the physical and chemical properties of carbon, which is its most important constituent, and in particular to the extraordinary combining powers of that element. The mystery of life, therefore, is the mystery of carbon.

G

These considerations would seem to have established the theory of spontaneous generation. By spontaneous generation is meant the non-parental origin of an organism—the rise of an organism, not from a previous organism, but from purely inorganic materials. Since precisely the same elements are found in both living and non-living matter, and since the only distinction between the two lies in the manner in which those elements are combined, there seems no reason for asserting that the more complicated organic compounds could not have arisen naturally and spontaneously, under the influence of chemical laws, just like the simpler inorganic compounds. In other words, there is no argument, which can be legitimately urged *a priori*, against the possibility of spontaneous generation. It must be admitted, that we have never yet succeeded in bringing it about by our own experiments. But as Haeckel truly says, each experiment with a negative result merely proves, that spontaneous generation is impossible under the very artificial conditions which we have supplied. In remote times there may have existed, indeed there must have existed, conditions very different from those which obtain at present. For example, the carbon now deposited in our coal-mines was once probably to be found in the atmosphere, the density and electric properties of which would, under those circumstances, have been very different. It is conceivable, however, that eventually the necessary conditions for the production of protoplasm may be hit upon, and spontaneous generation may then be proved experimentally to be a fact. For, contrary to general expectation, many complicated combinations of carbon, which chemists long despaired of manufacturing, are now produced artificially. Why not therefore, asks Haeckel, the most complicated of all?

Of course, it is only claimed by those who hold this view, that the *simplest* organisms have arisen through spontaneous generation. The sole organisms which could arise in this way, must be as perfectly undifferentiated and homogeneous as a crystal. These simple organisms, Haeckel thinks, began to appear when protoplasm first came into existence. Protoplasm resulted solely from the chemical combination of inorganic elements; and this combination probably took place originally at the bottom of the sea. The first living objects were monera, from which it is now asserted with considerable confidence that all organic life is but a development. The moneron, you remember, is a perfectly simple and structureless lump of protoplasm. The first step in its development would be the formation of a kernel or nucleus; and this may have taken place in a purely physical manner, through condensation. By this process the moneron becomes what, in physiological language, is called a cell; and the most perfect, the most complicated vegetable or animal organism, is merely a collection or community of such cells. The cells assume different forms and characters according to circumstances—according, for example, as they belong to the nervous or to the muscular tissue; but they are essentially neither more nor less than little nucleated lumps of protoplasm.

I shall point out to you hereafter, that if the existence of a divine mind and purpose be denied, this theory of development becomes involved in contradictions and absurdities. But there seems nothing unreasonable about it, if the existence of such mind and purpose be admitted. It is no more objectionable to the pious than to the scientific mind. To deny spontaneous generation is virtually to assert, that one of the many compounds of carbon, and one alone, has been miraculously produced. And it does seem antecedently improbable that, at this single point, the Creator should have arbitrarily interfered with the unity of nature and the unity of her laws of development. At any rate, it is easy to see which is the safer position for the theologian to adopt. The Church used always to assume that scientific doctrines would turn out to be wrong. But history teaches us that these doctrines have, for the most part, turned out to be right. Theologians have had to reconcile themselves and their theology to the movement of the earth, and to many other doctrines which they once looked upon as pre-eminently irreligious, but the truth of which it is no longer possible to doubt. The scientists were correct in their astronomy; why should they not be correct in their biology? We had better assume that they are, if we wish to place our religion upon an absolutely immovable foundation. I hope to show you by-and-by, that although the doctrine of evolution be valid, valid even up to the point of spontaneous generation, the grand old words are as true to-day as before the birth of science: "In Him we live, and move, and have our being."

It is because He is always with us, that we are sometimes apt to imagine He is nowhere to be found.

" ' Oh where is the sea ? ' the fishes cried,
   As they swam the crystal clearness through ;
' We've heard from of old of the ocean's tide,
   And we long to look on the waters blue.
The wise ones speak of an infinite sea;
Oh who can tell us if such there be ? '

The lark flew up in the morning bright,
   And sung and balanced on sunny wings,
And this was its song : ' I see the light ;
   I look on a world of beautiful things ;
But flying and singing everywhere,
In vain have I searched to find the air.' "

Agnosticism.

VIII.

EVOLUTION OF WORLDS.

WE have been engaged in taking a brief survey of the modern doctrine of evolution, in order that we may be in a position to answer the question, whether this doctrine is incompatible with the existence or knowableness of God. In the course of our survey, we have seen that there is no impassable barrier between species, but that the transmutation of one species into another, and the development of all existing species from a few primordial forms, may now be considered established facts. We have seen that there is no impassable barrier between plants and animals: for many objects have been discovered possessing the characteristic features of both; and therefore it is conceivable, not to say probable, that the entire vegetable and animal worlds may have been evolved from some single primary living creature. And lastly, we have seen that there is no impassable barrier between living and non-living matter: for protoplasm, the basis of life, is merely a peculiar combination of non-living elements; and many inorganic objects, for example crystals, present phenomena very similar to, and certainly not less mysterious than, the growth of organic bodies. The first living creature, therefore, from which the animal and vegetable worlds are supposed to have come, may itself have been an evolution from non-living matter. We have yet one further step to take, in order to reach the beginning of the present system of things.

I mentioned that protoplasm was probably first formed at the bottom of the sea. At any rate water of some kind is an essential part of its composition. It is because protoplasm contains a considerable proportion of water, that it is in the peculiar, semi-fluid state, which we saw to be the necessary condition of organic growth. Whence then came water? The complete answer to this question would be a complete history of the universe. Let us see now the way in which the evolutionists endeavour to explain, the origin of water upon the earth, the origin of that earth itself, the origin of the solar system, the origin of the stellar universe.

There was a time, they say, when our planet was destitute of water; at least the only water it contained existed in the atmosphere in the form of steam. Millions of years ago the earth was merely a confused mass of fiery vapour. But through the continual radiation of its heat into space, the temperature of this mass at last fell sufficiently for the fiery vapour to be reduced to the condition of a molten fluid; and by-and-by after more radiation the surface of this molten fluid cooled down into a solid crust. Then the steam in the atmosphere would be condensed and would fall as rain.

The evidence for this theory amounts almost to demonstration, and I suppose is more or less familiar to you all. (1.) The temperature of the earth's crust is found to increase as we descend, one degree for every sixty feet. A few miles down therefore, if the rate of increase continues, the heat would be sufficient to keep all known substances in a fluid state. (2.) Springs which rise from a considerable depth always possess a high temperature. (3.) In volcanic phenomena we have the eruption of large masses of matter in a fiery fluid condition. From all this it would seem to follow that the earth is still in a molten state, with the exception of a comparatively thin crust. This crust, as I said, was formed by the radiation of heat, from the originally incandescent surface, into the cold space of the universe. (4.) And the radiating process is still going on. Even after the rise of life, the temperature of the earth's surface was far hotter than at present. The temperate and frigid zones were once as hot as the torrid. For in the geological strata of the first and second periods we find, equally distributed over all zones, fossil remains of plants and animals which can now only live near the equator. In other words, the diminution of temperature which led to a distinction of zones and to a corresponding distinction in the habitat of organisms, only occurred in the tertiary period of geological development.

How came the earth to be so hot? The nebular hypothesis is an attempt to account for this phenomenon. This hypothesis was first put forward by Kant in 1755, on mathematical and astronomical grounds, and was afterwards supported, in a somewhat modified form, by Laplace.

Kant assumed that the entire physical universe was originally a gaseous chaos. He was led to this conclusion chiefly by the following considerations. When we examine the solar system, we find that all the planets and satellites move round the sun, not only in the same direction in which the sun revolves on his axis, but very nearly in the same plane. This common feature in the motion of so many different bodies, must result from some common cause, which either acts upon them now, or formerly did act upon them. At present there is no common cause which could compel the planets to take up the same direction of motion, for the intervening spaces are empty; in other words, they are disconnected bodies. But let us imagine that the planets themselves originally existed in such a diffused gaseous condition, as to fill the whole space now included within the widest planetary orbit, and then we have an explanation of their common motion, in the fact that they once formed part of a single body. The manner in which they now move separately, would be the result of the manner in which they once moved together. Kant then proceeded to argue back from our own solar system to other and older systems. The whole material universe, he thought, was once so much gas, existing in a state of very rare nebulosity—so rare that millions of cubic miles of it would only weigh a single grain. He assumed that this nebulous mass was in rotatory motion, and that its particles were under the influence of gravity—that is to say, that they mutually attracted one another. Owing to this attraction, the gaseous atoms congregated into gaseous groups, and these again into larger and larger groups, until at length the diffused nebulæ became split up into a number of smaller nebulæ,—relatively smaller, that is to say, but still of enormous volume. These masses were all in a state of intense heat from the previous shock of their atoms. Every such mass was the beginning of a solar system. Let us consider our own by way of illustration. When it first became a distinct body, the planets, as such, had no existence. There was but a single mass of diffused vapour, and from this planets were afterwards formed by the process of condensation. Some parts of the mass would be more dense than others, and would therefore attract to themselves the rarer matter which surrounded them. The large masses thus formed would similarly attract smaller masses, and this process would continue, till a few immense bodies had taken the place of the original cloud of gas.

Herschel was led to the same view by examining existing nebulæ, which he regards as worlds in the process of creation. Many of them seem to be composed of vast masses of phosphorescent vapour, and he conceived that these masses were gradually condensing, each around his own centre or around those parts which were most dense, and that the final result of this condensation would in most cases be the creation of a star. In different nebulæ he thought he could discover different stages of the process by which worlds are evolved.

Laplace's theory was much the same as Kant's, only he found himself obliged to start with a ready-made sun. He said it was mathematically certain, that if the sun had originally consisted of perfectly homogeneous matter, extending out uniformly to the orbit of Mercury, it would not have condensed into a globe, but into a flat, almost lens-shaped body. Laplace does not therefore attempt to go back to a purely nebulous mass; he starts with the sun at a time when he had an immense fiery atmosphere, filling the whole space now occupied by the planets. The sun, with its atmosphere, he conceived to have been in a state of rotation. As it cooled, it would contract towards the centre. This contraction of the central portion would, by one of the fundamental laws of mechanics, result in a faster rate of rotation. And owing to this faster rate of rotation on the part of the central mass, the exterior parts would become detached, and would be left behind in the form of a ring or zone of vapour. The same thing would happen again as the inner portion continued to contract, and thus a second ring would be flung off. So at last, instead of having a continuous atmosphere, the sun would be surrounded by a series of concentric rings. Each of these rings would be the beginning of a planet. As a rule some portions of the ring would be denser than others, and would gradually attract some of the rarer portions, so that at last a nucleus would be formed, round which the most rare and least attracted atoms would form an atmosphere of fiery vapour. This planetary atmosphere would behave just like the solar atmosphere; exterior rings would become detached, and would eventually condense into satellites. If the ring was perfectly uniform however—that is, if all parts were equally dense—no aggregate would be possible, and the ring would remain a ring, as is the case in the system of Saturn. Or we might have an intermediate case. There might be little masses of denser matter all over the ring, each of which would attract some of the vaporous matter to itself; and so the ring would be broken up into a group of small planets, like that which we see between Mars and Jupiter. And such of the materials of the solar atmosphere as were so rare and volatile as to be incapable of uniting to form either rings or planets, would continue to revolve around the sun, presenting an appearance like that of the zodiacal light.

Sir William Thomson gives a somewhat modified form of the theory. He starts with a chaos of stones and dust and gaseous matter, under the influence of gravitation. Suns and planets were alike formed, he conceives, by the falling together from enormous distances of portions of this *débris*. Each of the large bodies thus produced would be originally in an incandescent state. Some faint idea of the amount of heat caused by the concussion may be formed by reflecting on Helmholtz's calculation, that if our earth were brought to a standstill by a sudden collision with another body, it would be immediately fused and reduced to vapour. According to the theory of Sir William Thomson, it is easy to see why the sun is hotter than the planets. In the first place, the parts which formed it rushed together for that purpose from greater distances, and consequently generated more heat. And in the second place, the larger a body is, the longer it takes to cool; so that the sun, though lavishly spending heat from the beginning, will not be reduced to the earth's temperature for millions of years to come. Similarly in every other system of planets, the gravitating central body, being the largest, is also the dispenser of light and heat to its attendant worlds.

Now I think it is important you should notice, that Kant's is the only form of the nebular hypothesis which, in the strictest sense, is a theory of evolution. The problem of evolution is to show how the complex, the differentiated, the heterogeneous, has come from the simple, the undifferentiated, and the homogeneous. Laplace with his sun and atmosphere, Sir William Thomson with his stones and dust and gas, start from the heterogeneous, and do not therefore attempt a complete solution of the problem. Kant, on the other hand, did assume a perfectly homogeneous diffusion of gas throughout the space of the universe. But Laplace decided, on mathematical grounds, that if the sun had been evolved from matter in such a state of diffusion, it could not have had its present shape.

If you look at Herbert Spencer's 'First Principles' (chap. xix., on "The Instability of the Homogeneous"), you will see that the greatest authority on evolution only feels himself on safe ground when, like Laplace, he has got a comparatively heterogeneous state of things—viz., a central sun and an outside atmospheric envelope. He admits that the theory of evolution cannot give any definite account of the general structure of the universe. "The stars are distributed with a threefold irregularity. There is, first, a marked contrast between the plane of the Milky Way and the other parts of the heavens, in respect to the quantity of stars within the same visual areas. There are, secondly, contrasts of like kind in the Milky Way itself, which has its thick and thin places, as well as throughout the celestial space in general—the stars being much more thickly scattered in some regions than in others. And there is a third order of contrasts, produced by the aggregation of stars into small clusters. Besides this heterogeneity of distribution, a further heterogeneity is discovered when they are classified according to their differences of colour, which doubtless answer to differences in physical constitution. While the yellow stars are found in all parts of the heavens, the red and blue stars are not. There are regions in which the red occur in considerable numbers; others in which the blue are comparatively abundant; and others, again, in which both red and blue stars are rare. And one more irregularity of like significance is presented by the nebulæ, which are not dispersed with anything like uniformity, but are abundant around the poles of the galactic circle, and rare in the neighbourhood of its plane." "No one will expect," says Herbert Spencer, "that anything like a definite interpretation of this structure can be given, on the hypothesis of evolution or on any other hypothesis. The most that can be looked for is some reason for thinking that irregularities, not improbably of these kinds, would occur in the course of evolution, supposing it really to have taken place." The reason he assigns is what he calls "the instability of the homogeneous." Any finite mass of matter, he says, however diffused, and although perfectly homogeneous, must inevitably lapse into heterogeneity. For, setting external agencies aside, and supposing it to be the only matter in the universe, each unit of the homogeneous whole would be differently affected from any of the rest by the action of the rest upon it. For example, to put it roughly, a molecule at the surface of the mass would be very differently circumstanced, and under the influence of a very different set of forces, from a molecule in the interior. Motion therefore, and consequent change of distribution, must inevitably take place among the particles of the original mass. In matter of such extreme tenuity and feeble cohesion, there would certainly be motion towards local centres of gravity, as well as towards the general centre, just as particles of a precipitate aggregate into flocculi, at the same time that they sink towards the earth. These smallest and earliest local aggregations would be sure to split up into groups, which again would split up into other groups, each concentrating to its own centre of gravity. In conformity with the law that motion, once set up in any direction, becomes itself the cause of subsequent motion in the same direction, we may infer that the heterogeneities thus set up would tend ever to become more pronounced. And so even the most singular phenomena of all which the heavens present—

viz., their patchiness — might be expected *a priori.*

This is a bold, ingenious, and perhaps not altogether unsuccessful, attempt to justify the hypothesis of Kant. The mathematical difficulty however, as to the present shape of the sun, remains unanswered. And Herbert Spencer himself says, that "instead of committing ourselves to such far-reaching speculations, it will be better to descend to the more limited form of the nebular hypothesis which was enunciated by Laplace, and which assumes for the starting-point a sun, the nucleus of which is already globular in shape." Now, to start with certain definite materials arranged in certain definite ways, is really to admit the pre-existence of purpose and design. For out of these original materials there have been evolved (*ex hypothesi*) a world of order and progress; and our experience teaches us that order and progress do not result from accidental, but only from purposeful, arrangements.

But not to lay stress on this point, let us assume that the doctrine of evolution has been established, up to the extreme limit of perfect original homogeneity. Let us not at this moment stop to inquire whence came the first nebulous matter. Let us assume that it was there; and let us, without demur, make the evolutionists a present of the law of gravitation. What then? After we have admitted everything we have been asked to admit, there remains *just one half of the universe* — viz., the mental half, in regard to which evolution has not a syllable to say. If there was once a time when nothing existed but gas and gravitation, it is conceivable that there may have come into existence suns and planets, protoplasm and plants, animal organisms and creatures possessing the external semblance of ourselves; but out of gas and gravitation consciousness could never have been evolved. It shows the extraordinary one-sidedness of the physicists, that so many of them should set up the theory of evolution as a complete explanation of the universe, when, in regard to the whole of its most interesting and striking phenomena, that theory must for ever remain dumb. Consciousness they seem to look upon as a little detail in the development of things—a little, troublesome, inexplicable, unscientific detail — with which it is not worth their while to concern themselves. The world, they have explained to us, is a world in which evolution rolls on its silent way, eternally unseen and unnoticed. Its most marvellous results excite no attention, for there is no one to attend. There are creatures everywhere performing the functions of life, but they do not know that they live; not one of them has ever felt a pleasure or a pain; not one of them is capable of thought or imagination; not one of them has ever had a wish or experienced an emotion. They are all as unconscious as the ground upon which they walk. That is the only kind of world of which evolution gives a complete account. God save us from the stupidity of mistaking it for our own!

Agnosticism.

IX.

CONSCIOUSNESS.

WE have seen that the theory of evolution may be considered, within certain limits at any rate, to be an established fact; and that there are some reasons for supposing it to be true, even up to the extreme point of perfect original homogeneity. It may be that the whole material world has been evolved from a primordial cloud of gas. The whole *material* world, you will observe. But this leaves unaccounted for just one half of the universe—viz., the mental half. In regard to consciousness, as I said, evolution has not a syllable of explanation to offer. I must proceed to make this statement good.

Just think. You can conceive the development of complicated material structures from simpler forms of matter. You can conceive, for example, that the original cloud of fiery gas may have been split up under the influence of gravitation into several distinct masses of nebulous matter, and that each of these separate masses may have become a solar system, by throwing off rings of vapour which eventually condensed into planets. You can conceive that protoplasm may have been formed by the union, under chemical influences, of certain inorganic elements; that from protoplasm came, first monera, and then cells; that these cells multiplied by subdivision, and afterwards united together for the building up of complex vegetable or animal organisms; and that organisms have gone on developing into more and more complicated and perfect forms. But you cannot conceive that, from any combination of material atoms, immaterial consciousness has been evolved. A being conscious of his unity cannot possibly be formed out of a number of atoms unconscious of their diversity. Any one who thinks this possible is capable of asserting— to repeat my former illustration—that half-a-dozen fools might be compounded into a single wise man. Not even a single, isolated sensation can be conceived of as a mere evolution from matter.

This is sometimes admitted by the acutest of the agnostics. Call to mind, *e.g.*, some remarks of Tyndall's which I have already quoted: "The passage from the physics of the brain to the corresponding facts of consciousness is unthinkable. Granted that a definite thought and a definite molecular action in the brain occur simultaneously, we do not possess the intellectual organ, nor apparently the rudiments of an organ, which would enable us to pass, by a process of reasoning, from the one to the other. They appear together, but we do not know why. Were our minds and senses so expanded, strengthened, and illuminated as to enable us to see and feel the very molecules of the brain; were we capable of following all their motions, all their groupings, all their electric discharges, if such there be; and were we intimately acquainted with the corresponding states of thought and feeling, we should be as far as ever from the solution of the problem—How are these physical processes connected with the facts of consciousness?" This paragraph is quoted with approval by John Stuart Mill. Since then the passage from the brain to consciousness is unthinkable, it has not been thought by evolutionists. Since the connection between physical processes and sensations is an insoluble problem, it has not been solved by the evolutionists. They themselves being judges, consciousness is something which lies altogether outside the sphere of evolution.

Evidently then those who assert that modern physical science accounts for the whole universe, say what is not true. The insufficiency of the theory of evolution is curiously illustrated by several recent attempts to intellectualise matter. It is now often maintained by physicists, in a vague, indefinite way, that everything material has a mental side. At the close of his essay on "Scientific Materialism," Tyndall gives us an eloquent description of his musings on the summit of the Matterhorn: "Hacked and hurt by time, the aspect of the mountain, from its higher crags, saddened me. Hitherto the impression it made was that of savage strength; here we had inexorable decay. But this notion of decay implied a reference to a period when the Matterhorn was in the full strength of mountainhood. Thought naturally ran back to its remoter origin and sculpture. Nor did thought halt there, but wandered on through molten worlds to that nebulous haze, which philosophers have regarded as the source of all material things. I tried to look at this universal cloud as containing within itself the prediction of all that has since occurred. I tried to imagine it as the seat of those forces, whose action was to issue in solar and stellar systems and all that they involve. Did that formless fog contain potentially the sadness with which I regarded the Matterhorn? Did the thought which now ran back to it, simply return to its primeval home? If so, had we not better recast our definitions of matter and force? For if life and thought be the very flower of both, any definition which omits life and thought must be inadequate, if not untrue." There is a similar, and more frequently quoted, passage at the close of the Belfast Address. The Professor cites with approval Bruno's saying—" Matter is not the mere empty capacity which philosophers have pictured her to be, but the universal mother, who brings forth all things as the fruit of her own womb." "And," continues Tyndall, "believing as I do in the continuity of nature, I cannot stop abruptly when our microscopes cease to be of use. Here the vision of the mind authoritatively supplements the vision of the eye. By a necessity, engendered and justified by science, I cross the boundary of experimental evidence, and discern in that matter—which we in our ignorance of its latent powers, and notwithstanding our professed reverence for its Creator, have hitherto covered with opprobrium—the promise and potency of all terrestrial life."

Haeckel, also, talks very much in the same way in the preface to his 'History of Creation.' He, too, quotes a saying of Bruno, to the effect that "a spirit exists in all things, and no body is so small but it contains a part of the divine substance within itself, by which it is animated." Haeckel also quotes Goethe's remark that "matter can never exist and be active without mind." And he adds—"All bodies are equally animated; wherever there is corporeal substance, there is also mental power."

Similarly the late Professor Clifford, in an ingenious but highly illogical essay upon the nature of things-in-themselves, proceeding upon the double fallacy which I have before exposed—the fallacy, viz., of maintaining that feelings can exist without some one to feel them, and that a number of such impossible feelings, linked together in a certain complicated manner, will give rise to a self-conscious personality—

Clifford asserts that the molecules of matter, though devoid of mind, "possess a small piece of mind-stuff." In other words, every molecule is an unfelt feeling; and consciousness is just a combination of molecules which are individually unconscious.

Now the point to which I would call your particular attention is this. From the quotations I have just given, you will see it is admitted by many of the acutest agnostics, that the evolution of matter—in the ordinary sense of the term matter—would never have given rise to consciousness. They therefore tell us, parenthetically and incidentally, that when we talk of matter, we must remember something mental always goes along with it. It follows then, on their own showing, that the universe, as we know it, has not come from gas and gravitation alone,—using those words in their ordinary signification,—but from gas and gravitation *plus* something mental. Very well. That something mental I will not at present say *must*, but at any rate *may*, have designed and controlled the evolutionary development of the gravitating gas.

But it is constantly assumed by materialists that the proof of evolution is the disproof of God. And agnostics suppose that if the theory has not actually disproved the Divine existence, it has at least destroyed all positive evidence in favour of it. Let me show you how they argue.

The title of Haeckel's great work is, 'The History of Creation; or, The Development of the Earth and its Inhabitants by the Action of Natural Causes:' in other words—words which he uses in the first chapter—the book is intended as a "non-miraculous, non-supernatural history of creation." He distinguishes between the creation of matter and the creation of material forms. He says: "If we understand creation to mean the coming into existence of a body by creative power or force, we may then think of the coming into existence either of its substance or of its form. Creation in the first sense, —the coming into existence of matter—does not concern us here at all. This process, if indeed it ever took place, is completely beyond human comprehension, and can never form the subject of scientific inquiry. A naturalist looks upon the existing quantity of matter in the universe as a given fact. If any person feels the necessity of conceiving the coming into existence of this matter, as the work of a supernatural creative power—of the creative force of something outside of matter—we have nothing to say against it. But such a conception is an article of faith, and has nothing whatever to do with human science. The scientific history of creation is concerned only with creation in its secondary meaning—viz., the coming into being of the *forms* of material bodies. In this way geology, which tries to investigate the origin of the surface of the earth as it now appears, and the changes through which its crust has gone, may be called the history of the creation of the earth. In like manner the history of the development of plants and animals, which investigates the origin and changes of living forms, may be termed the history of the creation of organisms. As however in the idea of creation, although used in this sense, the unscientific idea of a Creator existing outside of matter and changing it, may easily creep in, it will perhaps be better, in future, to substitute for it the more accurate term development." "As to the much-talked-of purpose in nature," Haeckel continues, "I maintain it has no existence." Instead of the teleological view of the universe, he tells us he adopts the mechanical or causal view. Organic and inorganic bodies, he says, are the necessary products of natural forces. "We do not see in every individual species of animal and plant the embodied thought of a personal Creator; but the expression, for the time being, of the natural development of matter, the expression of a mechanical cause." The whole view of Haeckel may be summed up in a sentence from Lucretius: "Nature is seen to do all things spontaneously of herself, without the meddling of the gods."

Now my answer to Haeckel, and to the agnostics generally, is this. They fail to distinguish between two kinds of purpose—one changeable, the other unchangeable. With the latter—the unchangeable purpose—as I shall hereafter point out to you, evolution is not incompatible. On the contrary, that doctrine inevitably leads up to a Being, who is the same yesterday, to-day, and for ever. It is changeable purpose alone with which evolution is inconsistent. Evolutionists have taught us that the present system of things cannot be due to a purpose which continually contradicts itself. They have shown us that the development of nature is not interfered with by a capricious and changeable mind. And upon this important subject the world stood much in need of their teaching.

Men have too often made gods after their own image. Even civilised nations have frequently believed in a deity who was but a man "writ large"—a very indifferent, sixth-rate kind of man at best. Think, for example, of the old view of creation, which, owing to the authority of Cuvier and Agassiz, was long received as the orthodox doctrine. According to this theory, there were a series of quite distinct periods of creation, and each period had its peculiar flora and fauna. These periods were separated from one another by revolutions of an unknown kind, called cataclysms or catastrophes; and each revolution resulted in the utter extinction of the existing animals and plants. Afterwards a completely new set of organisms was created; and these remained on the globe for thousands of years, till they in their turn perished suddenly in the crash of a new revolution. Haeckel's caustic remarks upon this doctrine cannot be considered unjust. "According to this view," he says, "the Creator is nothing but a mighty man, who, plagued with *ennui*, amuses Himself with planning and constructing varied toys, in the shape of organic species. After having diverted Himself with these for thousands of years, they become tiresome to Him, and He destroys them by a general revolution of the earth's surface. Then, in order to while away

His time, He calls a new organic world into existence. At the end of thousands of millions of years, He is struck with the happy thought of creating something like Himself, and man appears upon the scene, who gives the Creator so much to do that He is wearied no longer, and therefore need not undertake any new creation." But perhaps men's thoughts of God never reached a lower point, than in the grotesque attempts which were made, during the middle ages, to account for the existence of fossils. It was, for example, seriously asserted that they were the rough models, which the Creator had first made out of mineral substances—models which he afterwards copied in the living organisms of animals and plants!

And much later than the middle ages, down even to the present century, the relation of the Creator to nature was often conceived of, in a way that was nothing short of blasphemous. Nature was thought to be so imperfect a production, that the Deity could only make it answer His purpose by constant intervention and readjustment. He had not foreseen the end from the beginning. Circumstances were always arising for which no provision had been made. He was everlastingly changing the course of nature; and, sad to say, He usually changed it for the worse. He was always seen in what was terrible and appalling. He had nothing to do with the beauty of an autumn evening, or the stillness of a moonlight night; with the merriment of youth, or the happiness of manhood, or the peacefulness of old age. In such cases things were but taking their normal course. But in agony, disaster, horror, men always recognised, as they thought, the finger of God. These were the unmistakable tokens of His presence. If the lightning struck a man dead, it was a sign that the Deity was angry. If an earthquake or a pestilence occurred, He was beside Himself with fury. Any peculiarly loathsome disease was technically called "a visitation from God." If a mother lost her darling child, it was because the Almighty was jealous that the poor little creature should have received so much of her love. The temper of this Deity, however, was fitful. You could never be certain what He would be at. Occasionally he forgot to be angry. In His ungodlike capriciousness He had favourites, for whose sakes He would sometimes work miracles of benediction. But this benediction generally involved disaster to those who were not His favourites. The many were plundered that the few might be enriched. And the favourites, having been selected by caprice, were almost sure sooner or later to be by caprice rejected. He would by-and-by repent Him of His choice. Altogether, His position in the universe was that of an eternal curse! If He had but let the world alone, it might have been a pleasant place enough, and men might have lived a happy life. But He would not let things be. He was always interfering, and always doing harm. Wherever He went, He left ruin and misery in His trail. He assumed many names, but His real name was Hate!

Now that is the kind of Deity whose existence has been disproved by the evolutionists. They have shown, once and for ever, that our world is not governed, or rather misgoverned, by omnipotent caprice. And for the establishment of this important truth, rational theology will be for ever indebted to them. To believe in evolution, is to be saved at least from the degradation of mistaking for God a purely imaginary being, who, if he really existed, would excite the hatred and the scorn of every noble-hearted man. How was it that men who believed in the omnipotence of a fickle fiend such as I have described, did not curse him to his face? It was because they were cowards. The falseness of their religion had so corrupted their moral sense, that, in order to keep out of hell, they were ready to barter their very souls. But never again, thanks to the evolutionists, will this terrible dilemma be repeated. Science has vindicated—unconsciously it may be, but none the less really—vindicated the character of the Deity from the aspersions which for ages had been cast upon it. And if now we believe in God at all, we find no difficulty in worship. The fact that in Him we live and move and have our being, is at once our deepest joy and our highest glory.

Agnosticism.

X.

PURPOSE *VERSUS* CHANCE.

WE have seen that the theory of evolution, as commonly understood and explained, leaves the mental half of the universe entirely out of account. In order to remedy this omission, Haeckel tells us to remember that matter always carries something mental along with it; and Tyndall suggests that we should recast our definition of matter, in recognition of the mental element it involves. We have, then, the authority of evolutionists for saying that the world has not been evolved from gas and gravitation—in the ordinary, vulgar acceptation of those terms—but from gas and gravitation *plus* something mental. And naturally it occurs to us to inquire, whether that something mental had anything to do with the evolutionary development of the gravitating gas.

It may be urged that the original something mental was but the *germ* of mind, out of which mind, as we know it, has been evolved or built up: in other words, that "the mind-stuff," to use Clifford's phrase, which originally existed, was of such a low and undeveloped type as to be incapable of purpose. I have elsewhere endeavoured to show the untenableness of this position.

But in the meantime let us take an *a posteriori* view of the matter. Here is a world said to have been evolved from gravitating gas. Is there any reason to think that this evolution was a divinely directed process? In other words, does nature give any evidence of supernatural purpose?

The agnostics generally say No; and, in justification of this verdict, they refer to the perfect regularity of nature. She bears no traces of capricious interference. The very changes which she undergoes take place according to unchanging laws. She cannot possibly, therefore, be under the control of a changeful purpose or a fickle will.

But purpose is not *necessarily* fickle. The

intentions of a reasonable being, just in proportion to his reasonableness, will be steadfast and fixed. To prove that nature bears no trace of the one kind of purpose, is certainly not equivalent to showing that she bears no trace of the other. Though she is not irregularly interfered with, she may be nevertheless regularly controlled.

And there is another important oversight, which you will generally find in the writings of evolutionists. They frequently assume that organisms have not been designed at all, because their various parts have not been separately and individually designed. It used to be thought, for example, that the eye, in every species of animal possessing that organ, had been in each case directly manufactured by God. Whereas we now know that any particular organ in one species, is merely an evolution from a somewhat different kind of organ in another species. But the absence of *particular* purpose is no evidence whatever for the absence of a general and all-embracing purpose. Though the eyes of animals have not been separately created, the possibility of vision may still have been intended to emerge in the process of evolution. Though the parts of nature may not indicate several purposes, the whole of nature may testify to one.

For this statement I am glad to be able to refer to the authority of Professor Huxley. In the 'Academy' for October 1869, he says: "No doubt it is quite true, that the doctrine of evolution is the most formidable opponent of all the coarser forms of teleology [those forms, viz., which suppose nature to indicate isolated, intermittent, changing, or incongruous purposes]. The teleology which imagines that the eye, such as we find it in man or one of the higher animals, was made with the precise structure it exhibits for the purpose of enabling the animal who possesses it to see, has undoubtedly received its death-blow. But it is necessary to remember that there is a wider teleology, which is not touched by the doctrine of evolution, but is actually based upon the fundamental proposition of evolution. That proposition is, that the whole world, living and not living, is the result of the mutual interaction, according to definite laws, of the forces possessed by the molecules of which the primary nebulosity was composed. From this it follows that the existing world lay potentially in the cosmic vapour; and that a sufficient intelligence could, from a knowledge of the properties of the molecules of that vapour, have predicted, say, the state of the fauna of Britain in 1869, with as much certainty as one can tell what will happen to the vapour of breath on a cold winter's day. Consider," Huxley continues, " the kitchen clock which ticks loudly, shows the hours, minutes, and seconds, strikes, cries 'cuckoo,' and perhaps shows the phases of the moon. When the clock is wound up, all the phenomena which it exhibits are potentially contained in its mechanism, and a clever clockmaker could, after an examination of its structure, predict all it will do. If the evolution theory is correct, the molecular structure of the cosmic gas stands in the same relation to the phenomena of the world, as the structure of the clock to its phenomena. So that the teleological and mechanical views of nature are not necessarily mutually exclusive. On the contrary, the more purely a mechanist the speculator is, the more firmly does he assume the primordial molecular arrangement, of which all the phenomena of the universe are the consequences; and the more completely is he thereby at the mercy of the teleologist, who can always defy him to prove, that this primordial molecular arrangement was not intended to evolve the phenomena of the universe." In other words, the phenomena of nature may be mechanically produced—produced, that is to say, without any intervention of will, and yet the mechanism which produces them may have been expressly designed for that purpose.

Very well. We have it, then, on the authority of Professor Huxley, that the original gas and gravitation *may have been intended* to produce the present system of things. What reason have we for thinking that they actually were so intended?

Everywhere around us there are what seem to be signs of purpose; and these appearances are multiplied ten thousandfold by scientific investigation. If you want to see how nature teems with contrivances, adaptations, expedients, mechanisms, read the works of Darwin. It is remarkable, too, that those who are loudest in denying the existence of purpose, are constantly using the very word which they declare to be illegitimate. Haeckel, for example, in the very book in which he says that "the much-talked-of purpose in nature has no existence," defines an organic body as "one in which the various parts work together, for the purpose of producing the phenomena of life." And this is no slip of the pen, as you will see from his description of the manner in which an organic body is built up. The most complicated animal or vegetable organism, he says, is merely a combination of the little nucleated lumps of protoplasm, called cells. The building up of an organism by these cells, he compares to the formation of a state. The simple cells, he says, at first exist in an isolated condition, each performing the same kind of work, and being satisfied with self-preservation, nutrition, and reproduction. "This condition of affairs corresponds to a community of human beings, as yet uncivilised. But at a later period in the history of evolution, the isolated cells gather themselves together into communities, and act like citizens who wish to form a state. Groups of simple cells remain together and begin to perform different offices. Some take to one occupation, some to another, and they all work together for the good of the whole. One set of cells devote themselves to the absorption of food; others form themselves into protecting organs for the little community; some become muscle-cells, others bone-cells, others blood-cells, others nerve-cells. By this division of labour it becomes possible for the whole state to accomplish undertakings which would have been impossible for the single individual. In short, various classes or castes arise in the cell-state, following diverse occupations, and yet working together for a common purpose. In proportion as the division of labour progresses, the many-celled organism, the specialised-cell community, becomes more perfect or civilised. But the vital phenomena of the most perfect organism, depend entirely on the activities of the cellular albuminous corpuscles." According to Haeckel, then, every cell in every organism gives distinct evidence of purpose.

But it may be urged that when scientific men speak in this way, it is because of the poverty of language, or through an occasional aberration of intellect, which leads them for the moment to adopt popular and erroneous views. It may be said that the conception of purpose is unscientific, and should be got rid of altogether. But I reply, the conception is not unscientific. The supposition that nature *means something* by what she does, has not unfrequently led to important scientific discoveries. It was in this way that Harvey found out the fact of the circulation of the blood. He took notice of the valves in the veins in many parts of the body, so placed as to give free passage to the blood towards the heart, but opposing its passage in the contrary direction.

Then he bethought himself, to use his own words, "that such a provident cause as nature had not placed so many valves without a design; and the design which seemed most probable was, that the blood, instead of being sent by these veins to the limbs, should go first through the arteries, and return through other veins whose valves did not oppose its course." Thus, apart from the supposition of purpose, the greatest discovery in physiological science might never have been made. Now, when the theory of evolution was less firmly established than at present, it was constantly urged in favour of it that, whether true or not, it was a good working hypothesis, and therefore scientifically valid. The supposition of purpose in nature, though it has not received, seems to me to deserve, at least as much respect.

At any rate, if the world be not due to purpose, it must be the result of chance. It is often asserted, I know, that it is due to neither, but is the outcome of law. But this is nonsense. A law of nature explains nothing, for it is merely a summary of the facts to be explained—it is merely a statement of the way in which things happen. The law of gravitation is *the fact* that all material bodies attract one another, with a force varying directly with their mass, and inversely with the square of their distance. Now the fact that bodies attract one another in this way cannot be explained by the law; for the fact is the law, and the law is the fact. To say that the gravitation of matter is accounted for by the law of gravitation, is merely to say that matter gravitates because it gravitates. And so of the other laws of nature; which, taken together, are the expression, in a set of convenient formulæ, of all the facts of our experience. The laws of nature are the facts of nature summarised. To say, then, that nature is explained by law, is to say that the facts are explained by themselves. The question remains, Why are the facts what they are? And to this question we can only answer — though the alternative is seldom recognised — either through purpose or by chance.

In favour of the latter hypothesis it may be urged that the appearances of purpose in nature have possibly been produced by chance. Arrangements which look intentional may occasionally be purely accidental. Imagine some one set to the task of drawing letters of the alphabet out of an infinite bag, into which they had been originally cast pell-mell. Every now and then he would get consecutive letters that would spell an intelligible word. On rare occasions he might draw out an intelligible sentence or paragraph. And it is often asserted that, given eternity to work in, along with an infinite number of nonsensical drawings, he might educe the poems of Homer or Shakespeare, or any other writer you like to name. Similarly, it is said our world may have been evolved by the accidental combination of atoms. In their haphazard collision they had produced, in past time and in far-off space, worlds which bore no sign of purpose, worlds where everything was irrational, monstrous, useless, and absurd. Nature does not know, and never did know, what she is about; neither does she care. She has never had the faintest conception of what would, or would not, turn up. Everything might just as likely have been something else. When life first appeared, it was a pure accident, lucky or unlucky, as we choose to regard it. The atoms once upon a time chanced to come together in such fashion that protoplasm was the result. The particles of protoplasm kept on subdividing, changing, and combining, during which process some living creatures became possessed of a mouth, while others obtained an eye or an ear, and so on.

By a continuance of good luck, animals in course of time grew more and more richly endowed. They came into possession of a variety of organs which, as it turned out, were capable of being usefully employed, till at last, after a splendid series of accidents, man himself appeared upon the scene. According to the chance theory, our world is only one out of an infinite number of possible atomic arrangements, all of which might have been considered equally probable beforehand. Chance, it is said, may just as easily have produced purposeful, as purposeless, appearances. *Something* was bound to come of the play of atoms; why not the particular world in which we find ourselves?

Why not? I will tell you why not. Those who ask the question forget that, so far as our experience goes, it is *only within narrow limits* that seemingly purposeful arrangements are produced by chance. And therefore, as the signs of purpose increase, the presumption in favour of their accidental origin diminishes. It is conceivable that words and sentences might, in course of time, be drawn accidentally out of a bag of letters. And if any one goes so far as to say, that the poems of Homer were produced in this fashion, I am unable to prove that they were not. Still I submit that this theory is unsupported by experience. Supposing it conceivable that a poem might be shaken out of a bag, I have never seen or heard of one composed in this fashion. And if the presumption against the accidental origin of a purposeful arrangement of letters, such as we have in Homer, be great, the presumption against such an origin for the whole of a country's literature is, of course, much greater still. What, then, must be the presumption against the chance origin of the purposeful arrangement of those material atoms of which the universe is composed? In a national literature we have myriads of combinations which seem to tell of design; but all the literature of the whole world is but a single item, a tiny detail, an infinitesimal fraction, in a universe which—in spite of all arguments to the contrary—still appears to be pervaded through and through with purpose. Let every human being now alive upon the earth spend the rest of his days and nights in writing down arithmetical figures; let the enormous numbers which these figures would represent—each number forming a library in itself—be all added together; let this result be squared, cubed, multiplied by itself ten thousand times; and the final product would still fall infinitely short of expressing the probabilities, against the world having been evolved by chance. Whoever believes in its accidental origin must have a singularly constituted mind. In comparison with such a supposition, the most extravagant vagaries of a theological fanatic, the wildest imaginings of a raving lunatic, are calm and sober sense.

Agnosticism.

XI.

THE INFINITE MIND.

WE have seen that the theory of evolution, as generally understood, while it may be a sufficient summary of material processes, leaves the mental half of the world altogether out of account. The ordinary evolutionist seems entirely to forget that there is such a thing as consciousness. Some however, Haeckel among the number, admit that matter always carries with it a mental element; and from this admission it follows, that along with the original gas and gravitation, from which the material world is said to have been evolved, there must have existed *something of the nature of mind;* and that therefore the process of evolution may have been designed and controlled by thought. That it actually was so designed and controlled, is rendered all but certain : first, by the fact that the ablest scientists cannot help recognising purpose in nature, notwithstanding their occasional assertions to the contrary ; and secondly, by the absurdities into which we are led, if we adopt the theory that nature is the outcome of chance.

But, say some, purpose could not have existed from the beginning. It has arisen, as have all the other attributes of a developed mind, during, and by means of, the process of evolution. The original mental something was the raw material, out of which consciousness has been evolved, just as the original gaseous vapour was the raw material of our present surroundings. Clifford tells us, in his 'Lectures and Essays,' that mind has been, so to speak, built up ; that it is composed of a number of elementary mental atoms. Every particle of matter, he says, carries with it a small piece of mind-stuff. When the material particles are combined in complex ways, the little pieces of mind-stuff that accompany them become likewise similarly combined, and the result is feeling, thought, mind, self-consciousness, personality.

Now, from what I have said to you on previous occasions, you will see that there is a fatal flaw in this ingenious theory. It fails to recognise the unity of consciousness. The distinguishing peculiarity of mind is to be one and indivisible. It remains persistently itself, while its experiences change and vanish. The particles of the brain are constantly wasted by use, and they are as constantly replaced by other particles. As they pass away, they must carry their pieces of mind-stuff along with them. Hence a personality is no more to be manufactured out of little pieces of mind-stuff, than out of little pieces of granite stuff. That which is one and permanent, manifestly cannot be a plexus of things which are many and transient. A personality cannot be compounded out of a number of impersonalities. Had we been made after Clifford's theory, whatever we had been conscious of, we should certainly not have been conscious of our own identity.

In opposition to Clifford's theory, it may be shown that a fully developed consciousness must have existed, before the process of evolution could begin,—that in matter, as we know it, there is necessarily implied the prior existence of an Infinite Mind.[1] And all the sciences con-

---

[1] See my 'Belief in God,' pp. 69-75.

tain the same implicit reference. Science, according to Bacon's well-known phrase, is " the interpretation of nature." To interpret is to explain; and nothing can be explained which is not in itself rational. Nature is interpretable because she has an intelligent constitution. And to say that her constitution is intelligent, is to say that she is dominated and suffused by thought. Thought can only grasp what is the outcome of thought. Reason can only comprehend what is reasonable. You cannot explain the conduct of a fool. You cannot interpret the actions of a lunatic. They are chaotic, irregular, contradictory, meaningless, absurd. It is only in proportion to a man's intelligence, that his actions bear an intelligible relation to one another. Similarly if nature were a mere chaos, an irrational system, there would be no possibility of knowledge. If the atoms were rushing aimlessly about, we could never discover what they were after, we could never foresee what would happen next. Even supposing they had by chance produced such a world as this, no reliance could be placed upon them. At any moment they might do something which they had never done before. At any moment the earth might vanish from beneath our feet, or in ten thousand other ways the prevailing arrangements might be suddenly reversed. There could be no course of nature, no laws of sequence, no possibility of scientific prediction, in the case of an irrational play of atoms. But as it is, we know exactly how the forces of nature act, and how they will continue to act. We can express their mode of working in the most precise mathematical formulæ. All the parts of nature are bound together by intellectual, and therefore intelligible, relations. Progress in knowledge consists in discovering the order, the law, the system, in a word the reason, which underlies material phenomena. Interpreting nature is neither more nor less than making our own the thoughts which nature implies. Scientific hypothesis consists in guessing at these thoughts; scientific verification, in proving that we have guessed aright. When, after many failures, Kepler at last hit upon the laws of planetary motion, he exclaimed, "O God, I think again Thy thoughts after Thee!" The discovery of these thoughts, it is evident, is not the creation of them. Science is but a partial copy of an intellectual system which existed long before the birth of man. Truth is not that which you or I may chance to believe. Devotion to truth is just the determination to give up our own individual fancies and predilections, to lay aside our own private and erroneous views, and to adopt the thoughts which are higher than ours — the thoughts, viz., of the Infinite Thinker.

One other question remains. Is the Infinite Thinker God?—that is, is He good? Experience answers, Yes. For the Power which is not ourselves, the Power which underlies ourselves and all finite things, unmistakably "makes for righteousness." There is no other fact so plain—no other fact in regard to which all intelligent men are in such complete accord. On this matter Hegel and Comte, the Archbishop of Canterbury and the President of the Royal Society, Mr Matthew Arnold and Mr Spurgeon, however differently they may express themselves, are in reality agreed. They all believe that, on the whole and in the long-run, it is not well with the wicked; that slowly but surely, both in the lives of individuals and of nations, good triumphs over evil. And this tendency towards righteousness, by which we find ourselves encompassed and hedged in, meets with a ready response in our own hearts. We cannot help respecting goodness; and we have inextinguishable yearnings for its personal attainment. Notwithstanding "sore lets and hindrances," notwithstanding the fiercest temptations, notwithstanding the most disastrous failures, these yearnings continually reassert themselves. We feel, we know that we shall always be dissatisfied and unhappy, until the tendency within us is brought into perfect unison with the tendency without us—until we ourselves also make for righteousness, steadily, unremittingly, and with our whole heart. What is this disquietude, what are these yearnings, but the Spirit of the universe in communion with our spirits, inspiring us, impelling us, all but forcing us, to become co-workers with Itself?

But I shall be told by the agnostics that this, after all, is only a kind of anthropomorphism; and by anthropomorphism is meant the degradation of the Almighty to our own level. Here, again, we may see the want of exactness in the so-called exact thinkers. They cannot be brought to distinguish between two totally different kinds of anthropomorphism. The one attributes to God what is lowest in humanity, and peculiar to it. The other attributes what is highest, and what, so far from being peculiar to ourselves, is essential to all intelligent and moral beings. Men have often, without doubt, ascribed to the Almighty their own evil passions, their own petty meannesses; and no words can be too strong for the denunciation of this kind of blasphemy. But the anthropomorphism which attributes to God such qualities as thought, purpose, consciousness, will, personality, is a very different matter; and yet the agnostics seem equally opposed to it. In his recent book on the 'Unity of Nature,' the Duke of Argyll says: "It is remarkable that the very men who insist most strongly upon our being one with everything beneath us, tell us at the same time that we are not one with anything above us."

You remember the passage I quoted from Professor Huxley, in which he says, that the original gaseous vapour may have been intended and adapted for the production of the phenomena of evolution, just as the mechanism of a clock has been arranged for the production of the phenomena of striking, showing the time, and so forth. But in the same article he goes on to tell us that the question, whether or not the process of evolution *has been* actually intended, is altogether beyond the reach of our faculties. "Let us suppose," he says, " a death-watch, living in the clock-case, to be a learned and intelligent student of its works. He might say, 'I find here nothing but matter and force and pure mechanism from beginning to end'—and he would be quite right. But if he drew the conclusion that the clock was not contrived for a purpose, he would be quite wrong. On the other hand, imagine another death-watch with a different turn of mind. He, listening to the monotonous tick! tick! so exactly like his own, might arrive at the conclusion that the clock itself was a monstrous kind of death-watch, and that its final cause and purpose was to tick; which, of course, it was not. Thus, the teleological theorist would be as wrong as the mechanical theorist among our death-watches; and probably the only death-watch who would be right would be the one who should maintain that the sole thing death-watches could be sure about was the nature of the clock-works and the way they move, and that the purpose of the clock lay wholly beyond the purview of beetle faculties." In other words, in our examination of the universe, we are like beetles examining a clock; and all our attempts at interpretation are sure to be wrong. But supposing that the beetle was, to use Huxley's words, "a learned and intelligent student," possessing sufficient intelligence to discover that the clock was a mechanism; then, although he might not understand all the purposes it had been intended to fulfil, and although he might sometimes be mistaken as to their relative importance, he would surely be justified in assuming that it had not been made by chance, that it had not been made for nothing, and that the intelligence of the mechanist who made it was, at all events, not inferior to his own beetle faculties.[1]

To sum up. All knowledge, whether practical or scientific—nay, the very existence of anything to know—is based upon, and would be impossible without, the existence of an Infinite Mind. And the tendency towards righteousness, which is so unmistakably manifested in the course of human history, together with the response which this tendency awakens in our own hearts, combine to prove that we are the children of a God. Further, this doctrine, though it glorifies man, does not in the least dishonour the Almighty. Though it does not fully express His nature, it is the most complete expression we are capable of formulating. Far removed as it is from being an adequate representation

[1] See also 'Belief in God,' pp. 80-82.

of God, every other view is infinitely farther from the truth.

And do not let us forget the practical importance of the subject we have been so long engaged in studying. Just as science consists in the free surrender of the mind, so religion consists in the free surrender of the heart, to the Power which is not ourselves. Just as it is the aim of the scientist to get rid of his own erroneous opinions, and to adopt the thoughts which are the thoughts of Nature, so you can only be religious by allowing your hearts to be possessed and ruled by a Love that is purer, by a Will which is holier, than your own. You must give up all that is mean and petty, all that is incompatible with the welfare of others and with the progress of the world. You must battle with your tendency to evil, you must cherish your aspirations after goodness. The burden of your prayer must be this: "Teach me to co-operate with Thee." You must lay down your life—the life which pertains to you as an isolated individual—and take up in its stead the infinite life of God.

PART II.

DISBELIEF IN IMMORTALITY: AS EXEMPLIFIED BY THE AUTHOR OF ECCLESIASTES

Ecclesiastes.

I.

INTRODUCTORY.

THERE is no book in the Bible which has been so variously interpreted as the book of Ecclesiastes. Commentators have taken not only different views as to its purpose, but views so diametrically opposed, that one can hardly believe them to be discussing the same treatise. Some, for example, have held that it was written by Solomon, in his old age, to prove his penitence; others, that he wrote it when he was irreligious and sceptical, during his amours and idolatry, and intended it as a justification of his wickedness. It has been thought, on the one hand, that the Messiah Himself specially inspired the author, for the instruction of His elect; and, on the other hand, the book has been regarded as the production of a profligate, who, in order to disseminate his infamous sentiments, tried to palm them off on mankind as Solomon's. According to some, the author of Ecclesiastes teaches that pleasure is worthless, and inculcates the practice of asceticism; while, according to others, he asserts that pleasure is the chief good, and exhorts men systematically to pursue it. Those who take the latter view are again divided among themselves; some of them maintaining that the author recommends a St Simonian licence in the pursuit of pleasure, others that he is in favour of a prudent self-control. One set of commentators have regarded the book as a philosophical treatise, possessing a definite unity of purpose; a second set have discovered in it a dialogue or controversy between several speakers, though they cannot agree as to which of these hypothetical persons is intended to represent the opinions of the author; while a third set of commentators see in Ecclesiastes only a medley of detached and heterogeneous fragments, culled from different writers and different ages. The book teaches the doctrine of Providence, say some, and describes the beautiful order of God's moral government, proving that all things work together for good to them that love Him. It teaches the doctrine of fatalism, say others, proving that all is confusion and disorder, and that the world is the sport of chance. It has been regarded as a disquisition on the *summum bonum*, as a manual of advice addressed to aspirants for political fame, as a history of the Kings of the house of David, as a pasquinade upon the career of Herod the Great. It has been held, on the one hand, to assert the immortality of the soul, and to urge on men the importance of setting their affections upon things that are above; and on the other hand, it has been thought to deny the immortality of the soul, and to urge on men the importance of setting their affections upon things that are below. It is designed, according to some, to comfort the unhappy Jews in their misfortunes; while, according to others, it contains the gloomy imaginations of a melancholy misanthrope, whose only message was despair. It has been considered by some so heterodox as to be unworthy of a place in the Canon, and by others so orthodox as to prove the doctrines of the Trinity and the Atonement.

We cannot be surprised that a book susceptible of such a variety of interpretations, should have been admitted into the Sacred Canon only after a long and protracted struggle. The question of its inspiration was hotly discussed by the Jewish rabbis. These rabbis are roughly distinguishable into two schools: the one, which was narrow and exclusive in its sympathies, led by Shammai; the other, which was broader and more cultured, led by Hillel. The narrower school maintained, that the book contained certain statements and sentiments which tended to lead men into infidelity: it could, they asserted, in no sense have come from God. The broader school, partly perhaps because they were fascinated by the Greek thought and culture traceable on almost every page, pointed out that, though it might contain much which was erroneous, it also contained much which was admirable and true. The broader school in the end prevailed, and succeeded in turning the balance of opinion in favour of Ecclesiastes, so that it was allowed to take its place side by side with all that was noblest and best in the literature of the Jews.

With regard to the authorship of the book, it used to be attributed to Solomon. This view is supported by the weight both of Jewish and Christian tradition; and the first voice of any importance raised against it was that of Luther, who supposed Sirach to be the author. Grotius was the next to deny the Solomonic authorship of Ecclesiastes, and he attributed the book to Zerubabel. Still, both Roman Catholic and Protestant writers continued to cling to the old view. Just before the beginning of the eighteenth century, however, fresh arguments were brought forward and urged with considerable force by Schmidt; and since then nearly all who are capable of forming an opinion on the subject have agreed that the traditional theory is false.

The most orthodox critics, such as Delitzsch and Hengstenberg, are on this point at one with the most heterodox. In fact, as Dr Ginsburg says, bringing forward arguments to show that Solomon did not write Ecclesiastes, would be considered on the Continent as much a waste of time, as trying to prove by syllogisms that the earth did not stand still. But as I am speaking in England, it may perhaps be advisable for me to make one or two further observations upon the subject. There is but a single reason for supposing that Solomon wrote Ecclesiastes— viz., that the writer speaks of himself (in ver. 1) as the son of David, and as king in Jerusalem; and (in ver. 16) as being celebrated for wisdom above those who had preceded him. These expressions manifestly point to King Solomon. But they do not prove that he wrote the book. They are quite compatible with the alternative, that the author had merely assumed the name and personality of Solomon. The Book of Wisdom, which the Church of Rome has recognised as canonical and the Church of England as semi-canonical, is entitled "The Wisdom of Solomon;" but no critic ever dreamed that Solomon was the author. It has always been a very common practice to write under a fictitious name; and in this practice there is no necessary imposture or dishonesty. It may be adopted merely as a means of attracting attention or exciting interest; and the author may feel perfectly certain that his device will be understood by all competent readers. While the study of medicine flourished in Alexandria, nearly every writer on the subject assumed the name of Hippocrates. Plato too, in his Dialogues, always gives us his own thoughts under the name of his master, Socrates. And there is no conceivable reason why a Scripture writer should have been debarred from forms of composition which others were at liberty to adopt.

Besides, the author of Ecclesiastes has himself helped us to see that he is but assuming the character of Solomon, for he represents him as belonging to the past. First, he says, "I *was* king over Israel." The past tense would be unmeaning in the mouth of the actual Solomon. Secondly, he compares himself (i. 16, ii. 7) to *all* that were before him in Jerusalem. This is an expression which the actual Solomon would not have used, since he had had but one predecessor in Jerusalem. That city, you remember, was only wrested from the Jebusites by David. Thirdly, the specification of Jerusalem as the seat of royalty, implies the division of the kingdom into two, which was subsequent to the time of Solomon, and after which there were two royal residences — one in Jerusalem and one in Samaria. Fourthly, he declares (ii. 18) that his successor—"the man who should be after him, the man who would enter into all his labour"—would be an utter stranger; "he might turn out a wise man, or he might just as likely turn out a fool." Solomon would not have spoken thus of his own son. Fifthly, the author of Ecclesiastes does not call himself Solomon, but he calls himself Koheleth; or, as our version has it, Preacher. The other reputed writings of the actual Solomon bear his name in their opening sentences. The Book of Proverbs begins with the words, "The Proverbs of Solomon;" and the Canticles with the words, "The Song of songs, which is Solomon's." But the author of Ecclesiastes, though he calls himself the son of David, and though he ascribes to himself some of the characteristics of King Solomon, does not adopt that monarch's name; he adopts the name of Koheleth.

This word is a participial adjective, and is feminine in form. It is intended to be in agreement with some word understood, and the most natural word to supply is "Wisdom." The verb from which Koheleth is derived means, to gather or assemble. It was a favourite custom with the Jews to personify Wisdom, and to regard her as having the power to gather together a circle of hearers. In Proverbs, for example, we read (i. 20), "Wisdom crieth without; she uttereth her voice in the streets: she crieth in the chief place of concourse, in the openings of the gates." The word Preacher then, which our Authorised Version gives us, is a mistranslation of the word which in Hebrew means gatherer, and which to a Jew would be a synonym for Wisdom. Hence it is evident that, though the author of Ecclesiastes describes himself in terms which suggest King Solomon, he wishes the reader to think, not of the actual monarch so called, but of Wisdom personified. In other words, he claims to be regarded as the embodiment of the learning of his time. The title of the book should be Koheleth or Wisdom, and the first verse should read—"The words of Koheleth, who is typified or represented by the son of David, king of Israel in Jerusalem." It will simplify matters if, in future, we call the author Koheleth, using that word as a proper name.[1]

So far I have been engaged in showing, that there is nothing in the book before us to prove that it was written by Solomon. I now pass on to point out that there is everything in the book to prove it was not written by him. The style is poor, quite unworthy of the Solomonic age; and the whole complexion of the treatise is totally different from that of any other canonical book. We could as easily believe, says Dr Ginsburg, that Chaucer was the author of 'Rasselas,' as that Solomon wrote Ecclesiastes. Besides, it contains a large number of expres-

[1] The word Ecclesiastes we get from the Septuagint. It means generally a member, but occasionally the convener, of an assembly.

sions, chiefly Aramaic, which are never found in Hebrew literature before the time of Malachi. If Solomon was the author of Ecclesiastes, says Delitzsch, there is no history of the Hebrew language.

There is another argument, too, of great weight against the Solomonic authorship. Ecclesiastes is saturated, as the Dean of Wells points out, with Greek thought and language. Let me give you a few illustrations. The phrase "under the sun," which occurs so frequently, is used in the sense in which the Greeks used it—to signify the totality of human life. In chapter iii. 21 (our version is here wrongly translated), Koheleth asks, "Who knoweth whether the spirit of man goeth upwards, and whether the spirit of the beast goeth downwards to the earth?" This phrase "who knoweth," both in regard to immortality and everything else, was the formula of Greek Pyrrhonism. In chapter x. 20, Koheleth says, "Curse not the king in thy thought, for a bird of the air shall tell the matter." This is a manifest reference to the Greek legend of the cranes of Ibycus.[1] The

---

[1] The story goes that the poet Ibycus was murdered by some robbers near Corinth; and as he was dying, he called upon a flock of cranes, that just then flew over his head, to avenge his

importance of opportuneness (what the Greeks called καιρός), of doing things in their season, on which Koheleth insists in chapter iii., had been taught in Greece by Chilon, Pittacus, Demetrius, Thaleseus and Theognis. The warning against excess in righteousness and in wisdom, which Koheleth gives specifically in vii. 16, had been given in general terms in the celebrated maxim, attributed to one of the seven sages, μηδὲν ἄγαν — nothing in excess. "The thing which hath been," says Koheleth, "is the thing which shall be; and there is nothing new under the sun." This is the Stoic notion that all phenomena, both in nature and in human life, happen in recurring cycles. The refrain of Ecclesiastes—" vanity of vanities "— is another echo from the Stoics. They had taken the same sad view of human life: they had called it "dust"; they had called it 'vapour"; they had called it "nothingness." Again, in the phrase "madness and folly,"

---

death. The robbers soon after went to a theatre, and during the performance some cranes made their appearance, and hovered over the heads of the spectators. Whereupon one of the murderers became so terror-stricken, that he betrayed himself by involuntarily exclaiming, "Behold the avengers of Ibycus." Hence arose the proverb as to a bird's love of scandal.

which Koheleth so often applies to human pursuits, we see the Stoic doctrine, that the vices and foibles of mankind were of the nature of insanity.

And there are in Ecclesiastes traces, no less striking, of the doctrines of Epicurus. These doctrines, as you know, are expounded at length in the poems of Lucretius and Horace. Now there are passages in Ecclesiastes which may be found, almost word for word, in Lucretius; as, for example, "The rivers run into the sea, yet the sea is not full." Both Lucretius and Koheleth, again, express similar views as to the dissolution of man's compound nature by death; as to our ignorance of all that comes after death; and as to our standing in that great crisis, for anything we know to the contrary, on the same level with the brutes. Lastly, some of the practical maxims which Koheleth lays down for the guidance of life, are the maxims of the higher Epicureanism, and remind one constantly of Horace. He points out, for example, that the secret of happiness, so far as happiness is attainable, lies in the cultivation of a cheerful temperament, in learning to be content with simple pleasures, and in avoiding the cares and annoyances which attend the pursuit of fame or wealth. "There is nothing better for a man," says Koheleth, "than that he should eat and drink, and make his soul enjoy good in his labour." "Live joyfully with the wife whom thou lovest, all the days of the life of thy vanity." "When goods are increased, they are increased that eat them: the abundance of the rich will not suffer him to sleep." All such maxims were born in Greece.

It seems certain, then, that Ecclesiastes could not have been written till the schools of Zeno and Epicurus had become prominent and influential—that is, not earlier than 250 B.C. The writer was, in all probability, a wealthy Jew, who spent his childhood in Palestine and his manhood in Alexandria. By the time at which this book was written, there had been a considerable amount of intellectual intercourse between Jews and other nations, and there was a growing tendency in Palestine to adopt foreign modes of thought and speech. For example, the distinctive name Jehovah was no longer used. Jews, like Greeks, now spoke only of God. But such a minute acquaintance with Greek thought and feeling as was possessed by Koheleth, can be explained only on the supposition that he had lived for a considerable time in

Alexandria, which was then the intellectual centre of the world. Koheleth, we must suppose, gave himself up first of all to pleasure; and afterwards, when that began to pall upon him, he devoted himself to philosophy and to thought. In his old age he wrote Ecclesiastes, in which he relates to us his experience and gives us his views of life.

His book may be considered in some sort a companion to the Book of Job. The subjects with which they are concerned are different, but correlative. Job was the most unfortunate of men, and he deals with the problem of misery. Is there anything, he asks, which can reconcile us to life at its worst? Koheleth, on the contrary was the most fortunate of men, and he discusses the problem of happiness. Is there anything, he asks, which can reconcile us to life at its best? Is life worth living? Is happiness worth having? Is our existence sublime or ridiculous, glorious or contemptible, a blessing or a curse? In the heyday of youth and health and pleasure, in the turmoil and excitement of the work of middle life, such thoughts do not often arise. But afterwards, when our sensibility to pleasure has been deadened, and our thirst for success has been quenched, then the questions which troubled Koheleth may trouble us. Are we satisfied? Have we any profit for all the labour that we have taken under the sun? Or have we been but embracing shadows? May our life be epitomised in the words vanity, emptiness, nothing?

Ecclesiastes.

II.

CHAPTER I. 1-11.

WE have seen that the book of Ecclesiastes has received an immense variety of interpretations. Most of them, however, violate the fundamental principle of literary criticism—the principle, viz., that an author's meaning is to be read *out of* his words, and not read *into* them. The majority of commentators have, first of all, determined what the author of Ecclesiastes ought to have said, and then they have set themselves to prove that he actually said it. I will give you a few illustrations of this style of interpretation. At the beginning of last century, F. Yeard, the Dean of Achonry, finding that the book contained several sentiments of which he did not approve, wrote a treatise for the purpose of showing that these sentiments had been really uttered by a refined sensualist, whom the author intended to represent as now and again interrupting and ridiculing the true doctrines. When anything strikes the Dean as improper, as falling short of his own more advanced beliefs, he says,—Oh, this must have been uttered by the refined sensualist. As soon as the sentiments become orthodox again, or what the Dean considers orthodox, they are supposed to be the sentiments of Solomon. Now there is nothing in the book itself to show, or even suggest, that it was intended to represent any such controversy. And it may be safely asserted that no rational writer would have mixed up his own doctrines with his opponent's in such a manner, that only the Dean of Achonry could tell us which was which.

The allegorical interpretations, of which there have been an enormous number, are all based upon a similar mistake. They all assume that the author ought to have written something else. They will not allow him to speak for himself; but they insist upon it, that when he is apparently saying one thing, he must really have been saying another. Both Jewish and Christian commentators have indulged very largely in this method of interpretation; and the consequence is, that folios and folios of nonsense have been written upon this book of Ecclesiastes,—a melancholy proof of the fondness of human nature for laboriously wasting its time.

In what are called the 'Midrashim Commentaries,' we have a collection of the opinions of the most learned of the rabbis. They have all allegorised Ecclesiastes in different ways—ways which have only the one characteristic in common, of never, even by accident, deviating into sense. Let us see what they make of it. In Ecclesiastes (i. 7) we read, "All the rivers run into the sea, yet the sea is not full." One rabbi says this means,—All people will join themselves to the Jews, and the number of Jews will thus continually increase. Another says it means,—All the dead pass into Hades, and yet there is room for more. Another interprets the passage thus,—All the Israelites go every year to Jerusalem, yet the temple is never crowded. And other rabbis have other equally absurd theories as to the meaning of the verse. Again, we read (ix. 14-16): "There was a little city, and few men within it; and there came a great king and besieged it, and built great bulwarks against it. Now there was found in it a poor wise man, and he by his wisdom delivered the city." Here, again, we have a vast variety of interpretations. First, the city is Sinai; the men are the Israelites; the king is the King of kings; the bulwarks are the six hundred and thirteen precepts of the law; and the wise man is Moses. Or the city is the synagogue, the men its members, the wise man its elder, and the King Jehovah. Or again, the city is the human body; the men are its limbs; the king is lust; the bulwarks are temptations; and the wise man is conscience; and so forth.

In the Targums we have a Chaldee paraphrase of the books of the Old Testament. The paraphrast of Ecclesiastes, with the coolest impertinence, foists upon Koheleth all his own favourite doctrines. For example, he believed in the influence of the planets. Koheleth must therefore have believed in it as well; and so the statement (ix. 2) that "all things happen alike to all," is translated thus,—Everything depends upon the planets; and whatever happens to any one is determined thereby. Again, the Targumist did not approve of Koheleth's doctrine about the future state; and he therefore substitutes a doctrine which he thinks more wholesome. We read (iii. 19), "That which befalleth the sons of men befalleth the beasts: as the one dieth, so dieth the other." This is paraphrased into,—The destiny of *wicked* men is identical with the destiny of beasts: as the beasts die, so die the impenitent.

There is the same fault to be found with the majority of Christian interpreters. St Augustine, for example,—having declared that the book was written to instruct us "concerning the life which is *not* vanity under the sun, but real under Him who made the sun," that is, concerning the spiritual life,—proceeds to interpret it accordingly. When Koheleth says, "There is nothing better for a man than that he should eat and drink," Augustine declares he is referring to the Eucharist. When Koheleth says, "Be not righteous over-much," Augustine maintains he is protesting against the Pelagian doctrine of works. Koheleth says (x. 16, 17), "Woe unto thee, O land, when thy king is a child, and thy princes eat in the morning! Blessed art thou, O land, when thy king is the son of nobles, and thy princes eat in due season, for strength and not for drunkenness!" In this Augustine sees a contrast between the kingdom of the world and the kingdom of Christ. The first is ruled over by the devil, who is called a child because of his foolishness and petulance; and men of the world are said to eat in the morning, because they take their pleasure in this life, which is but the dawn of their existence. The other kingdom is ruled over by Christ, who, being of royal descent, is styled the son of nobles, and His subjects eat in due season—that is, postpone their happiness till they come to the heavenly city. The eighth verse of the fourth chapter, though it ends with a declaration of vanity, is applied by Jerome to the work of Christ. The verse reads: "There is one, and not a second; he hath neither child nor brother: there is no end of all his labour; neither is his eye satisfied with riches." This refers, says Jerome, to the one Mediator with His one sacrifice, and to the fact that He is not satisfied with those already saved, but still endeavours to save more. When Koheleth states the simple maxim, "a threefold cord cannot be broken," Ambrose maintains he is referring to the tripartite nature of God, to the doctrine of trinity in unity. The allusion to the almond-tree (xii. 5), Peter of Lombard tells us, is a reference to the tripartite nature of Christ; the body, soul, and Godhead of Christ answering to the rind, shell, and kernel of the almond-tree. Koheleth says (i. 7), "The rivers run into the sea;" and this means, Richard St Hugo assures us, that the lusts of the flesh, though pleasant at first, always end in brackishness. And so the explanations go rambling on down to 1659, when they culminate in Dr Gell's suggestion that, in the words, "Live joyfully with the wife whom thou lovest," we are exhorted to give ourselves up to the pleasures of memory. "The wife here," says Dr Gell, "means our memory and thoughts; and an excellent portion it is in this vain life that with our wife —that is, with our memory and thoughts—we may see and enjoy the divine life." "Unless in this manner," he adds, "we understood the advice of Solomon, an epicurean might make use of it to confirm himself in his voluptuousness." But why it was impossible for Koheleth to express any sentiments disapproved of by Dr Gell, does not appear.

Now these are examples of the kind of interpretation we must avoid. You see, of course, the objection to this method of criticism. If a threefold cord may mean the Trinity, it may also mean anything in the universe which is capable of being divided or distinguished into three. If the term wife may mean memory, it may just as well mean imagination, or faith, or hope, or any other faculty or activity of the mind. This kind of criticism, by which everything may be extracted out of anything, and anything may be elicited from nothing, however ingenious, is dishonest and irreverent: dishonest, for it is an attempt to obtain, unfairly, confirmation for our own opinions; irreverent, for if a book be worth reading at all, it is our business to try and learn the author's views, and not to teach him ours.

And now let us proceed to study Ecclesiastes for ourselves. The book which Koheleth wrote, ended, we may be sure, with the eighth verse of the twelfth chapter. What follows is a postscript, added by a commentator. In verses 9 and 10 we have notices of Koheleth's other writings; in verses 11 and 12, remarks on the general usefulness of such writings; and in verses 13 and 14, a *résumé* of the commentator's religious views. The first verse of the book is, properly speaking, the title. Koheleth's treatise, therefore, begins at i. 2, and ends at xii. 8. It opens with the words, "Vanity of vanities, saith Koheleth, all is vanity," and with these words it concludes. The utter vanity of life,—the form in which this is expressed ("vanity of vanities") being the strongest Hebrew superlative,—the utter vanity of life is the fundamental idea of the writer, and it is constantly repeated as a melancholy refrain. The book is a kind of soliloquy upon this text, interspersed with those practical observations and suggestions, the observance of which, the author thinks, might tend to make life, if not happy, at least endurable. Koheleth seems to have put down his thoughts pretty much as they originally suggested themselves. "He was not," says Dr Samual Davidson, "so far as we can judge, an adept in writing." There are digressions and repetitions and contradictions which, though they may be very suggestive to the thoughtful reader, detract from the merit of his treatise, considered as a piece of literature or work of art.

Koheleth begins his soliloquy with the thought that we are not immortal. *What profit* hath a man, he asks, for all his labour that he taketh under the sun? or, according to the Hebrew, What is there that remains to a man of all the toil that he toileth? What has he to show for it at last? One generation passeth away, and another generation cometh. Men are only born to die. It is not so with the world in which men live; the earth abideth for ever. Everywhere around us we see change, and yet renewal. The sun sets and rises again; the winds blow continually on their appointed courses; the rivers flow into the sea, but they return, through fissures and crevices in the rocks, and so form fresh rivers. The phrase that is rendered (verse 8) "All things are full of labour," should be translated, " All words are feeble "—*i.e.*, feeble to express the truth, on which Koheleth has just been insisting, as to the eternal recurrence of nature's phases. Illustrations of it are innumerable, and objects in nature which confirm it are omnipresent, so that the eye however curious, the ear however inquisitive, could never apprehend them all. The earth is possessed of perpetual youth, and she continually repeats herself. What she is doing now, she has done in time past, she will do again in time to come. The thing that hath been is that which shall be, and there is nothing new under the sun. The earth is the same yesterday, to-day, and for ever. But how different it is with man! Generation after generation passeth away, and returneth never more. We do not live even in the memory of our fellows. There is no remembrance of former men [not "things," as our verse has it]; neither will there be any remembrance of those that come after us. Our successors, as well as ourselves, must pass into everlasting oblivion. Sooner or later men are doomed to be forgotten. "The name of Echebar," says Jeremy Taylor, "was thought by his subjects to be eternal, and it was believed that all the world did not only know but fear him: but ask, here in Europe, who he was, and no man hath heard of him; demand of the most learned, and few shall resolve you that he reigned in Magor.' There are some, it is true, who have been more widely known, and whose fame has lasted longer, than this once celebrated king. Horace, you remember, says in his last ode, with the grand self-assurance of a genius, "I shall not altogether die. I have completed a monument more lasting than brass, loftier than the regal structure of the Pyramids." He was right; he has lived for nineteen centuries already, and will probably survive for much more than nineteen centuries to come. But by-and-by—unless we are immortal—his name must be lost; for by-and-by the human race will have perished, and carried with it the name of Horace into "the land where there is no remembrance."

"But the earth abideth for ever." This was

what angered Koheleth—that man should perish, when the world in which he lived was eternal. And, apart from immortality—that is to say, from Koheleth's point of view—all that he said two millenniums ago, may be repeated with equal correctness to-day. We know, it is true, that the earth cannot remain always just where and what it is. We know that worlds, like human beings, pass through various stages of development and decay. But *in contrast to man* the earth may still be considered as comparatively everlasting. Moreover, what Koheleth called the earth, we in these days should call nature; and in the system of nature, as we understand it—that is to say, in the universe considered as a whole—the birth and death of worlds are regular, ordinary occurrences, taking place at stated intervals according to definite laws, and illustrating in the most striking manner that persistent recurrence of natural phenomena, which had excited the attention and the envy of Koheleth. If, as modern science teaches, space be infinite, and matter be scattered everywhere throughout the universe, all the processes of nature, including the origin and dissolution of worlds, must be in the strictest sense eternal. One generation passeth away and another generation cometh; by-and-by the last generation of our race will appear, and disappear like the rest into nothingness. But nature will then be as young as she is to-day. Nature abideth for ever.

> "The years no charm from Nature take;
> As sweet her voices call,
> As beautiful her mornings break,
> As fair her evenings fall."

Koheleth had probably gone to Alexandria in his youth, just as wealthy foreigners in the present day come up to Oxford or Cambridge. He started in his career with a thirst for pleasure, but with a still greater thirst for wisdom. He would enjoy himself, he resolved; but he would also study. He would learn all that the Alexandrian philosophers could teach him; he would become an original thinker; he would make himself famous; he would be acknowledged as wiser than any one who had been before him. And now, towards the close of his life, when his most cherished hopes had been fully realised, when his brightest dreams had been actually accomplished, it suddenly occurred to him that he must die. And what then? Will anything remain to him as a permanent possession? He thinks not. He believes that he will then be as though he had never been. Having come to this conclusion, he falls into the melancholy soliloquy, of which the book before us is the expression. And it seems to me, that whoever takes Koheleth's view of human destiny, should participate in Koheleth's despair. What avails it to be a Homer or a Cæsar to-day, if to-morrow I am to be but a heap of dust?

> "Weighed in the balance, hero dust
> Is vile as vulgar clay."

Ecclesiastes.

III.

CHAPTERS I. 12—III. 22.

WE have seen that Koheleth was led into his melancholy soliloquy, by the thought that he must pass away and be no more; and that he mournfully contrasted the brevity of human existence, with the permanence and seeming eternity of nature.

He now mentions the unusual advantages which he had possessed, for enjoying life and making the best of it. "I, Koheleth, was king over Israel in Jerusalem." His opportunities could not have been greater, he considers, had he been Solomon himself. He henceforth speaks, therefore, under the personated character of the wise son of David. He speaks as one who represents the wisdom and prosperity of his age.

I have given my heart, he says, to seek and search out by wisdom concerning all things that are done under heaven; or, as we should express it, I have set myself to the task of investigating scientifically the value of all human pursuits. This, he assures us, is no pleasant work. It is "a sore travail that God has allotted to the sons of men," which they cannot altogether escape. There comes a time in the life of every man when the question forces itself upon him,—what is the good of it all? Some men never give a definite answer to the inquiry; they try to forget it by devoting themselves with increased ardour to pleasure or to work. But not so a man like Koheleth. It is the doom of the thinker that he must think, even though his thinking drives him to despair. Koheleth thought, and thought, and thought, till he was forced to the conclusion that all human pursuits —all the works done under the sun—were vanity and vexation of spirit, or, according to the literal Hebrew, were but vapour and striving after the wind. There was no solidity, nothing permanent, nothing enduring, about human possessions or achievements. For man was doomed to pass away into nothingness.

Instead of crooked (i. 15), we should read desponding—"The desponding cannot be set right; for those who have died cannot again be numbered (with the living)." Nothing, he means to say, can remove his despondency; for the dead can never be recalled to life.

In verse 17 we should read, instead of madness and folly, the word knowledge—"I gave my heart to know wisdom and to know knowledge." The phrase madness and folly must have crept in through a transcriber's error. It has no connection whatever with the context. Koheleth is speaking of the knowledge of life which he has acquired, and of wisdom, which he uses as a synonym for it. This is proved by verse 18, where he speaks, not of wisdom and madness and folly, but of wisdom and knowledge.

I have gotten, he says, more wisdom than all that have been before me. I have had the most varied experience. I have done my very best to learn the art of life. And what is the result? Only vexation of spirit. In much wisdom is much grief; and he that increaseth knowledge increaseth sorrow. I, Koheleth, who have taken the utmost pains to ascertain the value of existence, have been forced to the conclusion that it is not worth having.

Having stated his position in these general terms, he now enters into the subject a little more in detail. He reminds himself how, at one time, he had tried to find his happiness in pleasure and amusement. But pleasure had palled upon him and appeared good for nothing; and as for amusements, well—like Cornewall Lewis—Koheleth thinks that life might, perhaps, be tolerable without them. But he who expects to be made *happy* by them, must be mad. He reminds himself that he sometimes had recourse to wine, in order to stimulate his jaded body, and that "he laid hold on folly"— that is, adopted any expedient however seemingly absurd—rather than lose the chance of increasing his enjoyment. All the while, he assures himself, he had been acquainting his heart with wisdom—that is to say, he did what he did by way of scientific experiment, in order that he might see whether there was anything really worth man's while to do during the numbered days of his life. He pursued his investigations on the most magnificent scale. His possessions and surroundings were those of a prince. He built houses for himself in town and country; he planted vineyards; he laid out parks; he erected reservoirs for artificial irrigation; he had an immense number of retainers; his revenue was equal to a king's; the best that the age could produce in music and other forms of art was all at his disposal; the members of his harem were carefully selected from every clime and country; his prosperity kept on increasing, till at last he seemed to be more fortunate than any other of the sons of men. And all this time, as he tells us again, his wisdom remained with him. He was not the slave of his possessions or of his pleasures, but their lord. He kept steadily before his mind the fact that he was making an experiment, that he was seeking after the *summum bonum*. In all his indulgences, therefore, he exercised a prudent relf-restraint; but, at the same time, he never relaxed in his pursuit of happiness. He left no expedient for attaining it untried. "Whatever mine eyes desired," he says, "I kept not from them. I withheld not my heart from any joy." The latter part of verse 10 is mistranslated. Instead of "my heart rejoiced in all my labour; this was my portion of all my labour," it should be, "my heart was to rejoice in all my labour; this was to be my portion of all my labour." That is to say, enjoyment—the maximum of enjoyment—was the end he had in view. He put into requisition every conceivable expedient for obtaining it, and what was the result? In a cool moment he asked himself if he was happy, and he was constrained to answer, No! I looked, he says, on all the work that my hands had wrought, and on the labour that I had laboured to do; and behold all was vanity and vexation of spirit, and there was no profit under the sun. All is but vapour and striving after the wind. All passes away into nothingness.

> "Though man's life be a dream, his pleasures, I see,
> Have a being less durable even than he."

Having discovered the unsatisfactoriness of pleasure, Koheleth goes on to inquire if there is anything else that could take its place. What of wisdom? Can that make life a desirable possession? He proceeds to institute a comparison between wisdom and pleasure. No one, he tells us, is better able to do this than himself. I turned, he says, to consider wisdom and madness and folly,—madness and folly being a form of expression derived from the Stoics, who used it as a synonym for pleasure. I considered wisdom and pleasure; and I saw that there is profit in wisdom more than in pleasure, just as light is superior to darkness. Pleasure is but momentary, wisdom may last for a lifetime. Pleasure is but a shadow, wisdom is comparatively substantial and real. The lover of pleasure is like a blind man: he cannot distinguish between substance and shadow; he cannot see the beauty of wisdom, and knows not where she is to be found. The lover of wisdom, on the contrary, has seen her, and will follow her till he dies. Ay, there's the rub,—till he dies. One event happeneth to them all. The wise man must die, and sooner or later be forgotten, just like the fool. What then, after all, is the good of wisdom? This, too, is vanity. And not only must the wise man die, but he must leave his possessions behind him, to be inherited, very probably, by a fool. O the pity of it! To think, says Koheleth, of a fool having command over all my property, in the acquisition of which I showed myself so wise. The possessions amassed by much toil and skill, [the word rendered equity (ii. 21) means skill], will be speedily dissipated by the reckless folly of the fool. At the thought of this crowning calamity, says Koheleth, I hated life; I hated all the occupations of life; I gave myself up to despair. What *hath* man for all his labour and for the vexation of his heart? What is the result of his persevering efforts and of his corroding anxiety? Nothing but disappointment—disappointment of which he is conscious all day long, and which he scarcely forgets even in the night. It haunts his very dreams.

Since, then, wisdom and pleasure are both evanescent, let us, he says, choose pleasure, because it is the more agreeable. Since we cannot secure anything that will abide with us in the future, there is nothing better for us than to eat and drink and enjoy the present as much as we possibly can. But we must remember, that enjoyment does not come most to him who seeks most for it. We may be too eager in its pursuit. Those elaborate experiments of his, he now regards as a profound mistake. Happiness is "from the hand of God;" it is not to be achieved by direct effort. To the sinner, to the man who is greedily, unscrupulously bent on gathering wealth and heaping up treasures, God gives only disappointment. But to the good man, to the man who listens to the voice of conscience, and who is content with simple pleasures, God giveth wisdom and joy. Such a man has learnt the art of life; he may be called happy. But after all (and here he returns to his old sad thought) even this wisdom and joy that come from the hand of God, and are the rewards of a well-spent life—the deepest wisdom and the intensest joy we can ever hope to obtain—even these are but poor things at best. They are also vanity.

In the third chapter Koheleth points out, how anything like success in life must depend upon our doing the right thing at the right time. There is a fitting season for everything, and woe be to us if we miss our opportunity! Inopportuneness is the bane of life.

> "There is a tide in the affairs of men
> Which, taken at the flood, leads on to fortune;
> Omitted, all the voyage of their life
> Is bound in shallows and in miseries."

What we have to do is to watch for our opportunity and embrace it. He points out (verse 11) that these opportunities are of divine appointment. It is God who hath made everything beautiful in its season. We cannot create opportunities; we can only accept them.

But, after all, what is the good? We are in reality no better off in the end, if we availed ourselves of a favourable chance, than if we had missed it altogether. What profit hath he that worketh in that wherein he laboureth?

I have had, says Koheleth, a wide experience in the fruitlessness of human efforts, in that useless toil which God hath allotted to men as their miserable doom. Success is no better than failure. For God hath set eternity in our hearts; [so the word "world" in the 11th verse should have been rendered.] There is something in our hearts that makes us dissatisfied with the present, something that compels us "to look before and after." But though we are compelled to *look*, we are prevented from *seeing*. No man can find out the work that God doeth, from its beginning to its end. We only know parts of His ways; we can never comprehend the whole. We cannot decipher the mysteries of Providence. We cannot discover what the Deity is about. Why do we trouble ourselves with such high questionings? Let us leave them. Though eternity has been set in our hearts, we must learn to forget it, if we are ever to have any peace. The best thing for us, Koheleth says again, is to eat and drink, and somehow or other, any way we can, to extract enjoyment out of the common occupations of life. [The words "do good," in verse 12, should be "do himself good."] Since we cannot tell anything about what is beyond, let us seize upon the present and enjoy it. This must be the divine intention, or, as he calls it, the gift of God. We have just the same sentiment, you remember, in one of Horace's odes. While we are troubling ourselves about the future, the anxious hours are stealing from us our chances of enjoyment. Let us make the most of to-day, says Horace, and let the future take care of itself.

Koheleth seems now (iii. 14) to rise for a moment into a religious mood. But his religion, as we shall see a few verses further on, is by no means of an exalted type. Times, seasons, and opportunities, he says, are of divine appointment; and, like nature's phases, they happen in recurring cycles. Whatever God doeth, it is eternal; He recalls the past. Times and seasons repeat themselves, and, in their occurrence and recurrence, we ought to recognise a higher Power. God doeth it that men should fear before Him. The existence of so much unrequited wickedness in the world, might seem to suggest that there was no higher Power. But there is. God *will* judge the righteous and the wicked, and reward them according to their works. There is a time for every purpose and for every work, and therefore for the purpose of retribution among the rest. Retribution is delayed for the sake of showing men that they are, in the sight of God, of no account. God is determined they shall see themselves to be but beasts.

And they *are* but beasts. As the one dieth, so dieth the other. They have one spirit. Man has no advantage; for both beast and man are vanity. The earlier part of verse 19, which in our version reads—" That which befalleth the sons of men befalleth beasts, even one thing befalleth them," if literally translated, would be —" Chance are the sons of men; chance is the beast; both are subject to one chance." In other words, the life and the death of beasts and of men are but chances, accidents, trifles, matters of no moment whatsoever in the great universe of God. All are of the dust; all turn into dust; all go to one place; the earth is the mother and the sepulchre of all. The 21st verse, again, is wrongly translated. Instead of, " Who knoweth the spirit of man that goeth upward, and the spirit of the beast that goeth downward," we should read, " Who knoweth whether the spirit of man goeth upward, and whether the spirit of the beast goeth downward to the earth?" There *may be* a difference, it occurs to him. The spirit of man may be something more than dust. Perhaps it is. Who knows? However, life cannot be based upon a "perhaps." We must draw away our thoughts from all such fancies, and fix them upon what is real. There is no mistake about pleasure; that is pleasant while it lasts. I perceived, he says, there is nothing better for a man than pleasure. That is his true portion. That is his only chance. No one can tell him anything for certain about the next world; therefore let him enjoy this.

An ignoble doctrine, but still not unnatural. Having struggled in vain to solve the problem of existence, a man is tempted to give it up in disgust, and say to his soul,—Poor soul! take thine ease and rest thyself after thy fruitless questioning; give thyself to enjoyment. But, thank God! the soul will not take its ease; it will not rest itself; it will not be lulled into apathy. It reasserted itself again, as we shall see, in the case of Koheleth; and it forced him to the same conclusion to which we are all sooner or later driven. However much in the dark we may feel ourselves, as to the meaning of our present existence, or as to the kind of destiny that lies before us in the future, there is one lesson which experience cannot fail to teach us, and it is this,—we have been endowed with a nature which is too great to be satisfied with pleasure.

Ecclesiastes.

IV.

CHAPTERS IV. 1—V. 7.

WHEN we last parted from the author of the book of Ecclesiastes, he had arrived at the conclusion that the chief purpose of life was enjoyment. Death, Koheleth thought, made an end of men, just as it made an end of beasts; or if not, if there were a difference between us and the brute creation, we could never hope to obtain any certain knowledge upon the subject. We can discover neither the meaning of our existence, nor the destiny that lies before us in the future, and therefore the best thing for us is to drink, systematically and continuously, from the fountain of pleasure. He says in effect with the Persian poet Omar Khayyam:

"Drink! for you know not whence you come, nor why;
Drink! for you know not why you go, nor where."

But in such a doctrine as this no thoughtful man can rest. Koheleth practised it for a time, and found it to be a failure. In the fourth chapter he comes to the conclusion that life is essentially and irretrievably wretched—wretched, not because (as he had formerly thought) it would so soon be over, but wretched, because it lasted so long. Once he complained that men died too soon: now he complains that they do not die soon enough. All that pleasure did for him was thus to increase his gloom. There was one thing he had forgotten in making out his programme—he had forgotten the miseries of other people. The prosperity he secured for himself did not remove their adversity, but only brought it out into more startling relief. He was infected by their wretchedness; for, in the midst of all his dissipation, he had preserved a kindly heart.

I considered, he says, the tears of those who are oppressed and who have no comforter. The oppression of the poor by the rich was one of the most characteristic phases of oriental society. To be poor was to be weak, and to be weak was to be reduced more or less into the condition of a slave. Koheleth's own countrymen had suffered much from the cruelty of foreign despots. There is a reference also, in this verse, to another characteristic of Eastern society. It is customary to pay formal visits of condolence to afflicted friends. People travel great distances in order, as they express it, to comfort the mourners. To have no comforter, therefore, means to be friendless. The thought of the vast masses of mankind who were in this lonely and down-trodden condition, made Koheleth so wretched that he wished he was dead —wished he had never been born. I accounted, he says, the dead—who died so long ago as to have been by this time altogether forgotten —I accounted them happier than the living. And happier still would it have been, never to have come into the world at all—never to have seen the evil deeds that are done under the sun.

It is a curious transition this, through which Koheleth has passed. From deploring the shortness of life, he has come to deplore its length. Wretchedness, he now thinks, is unavoidable. If we have no calamities of our own, we shall still suffer in the calamities of others. The same sentiments have been often expressed before and since. Herodotus, *e.g.*, relates that when Xerxes was invading Greece, he thought he would like to look at the whole of his forces at once. He therefore ascended a hill, from which he could see the Hellespont crowded with his ships, and the plains swarming with his troops. At the sight he burst into tears; and he apologised for his emotion to one of his generals by saying, "There came upon me a sudden pity, when I thought of the shortness of man's life, and considered that of all this host, numerous as it is, not one will be alive when a hundred years are gone by." "And yet there are sadder thoughts than that," replied the general; "short though our life is, it appears too long when sickness or calamity falls upon us; and death then seems a most sweet refuge."

In verse 4, Koheleth makes a new departure. He surveys human life afresh, from another point of view. He remarks that greed is at the bottom of a good deal of human misery. All work, he says, and all dexterity in work [the "right work" of our version means really dexterous or skilful work]—all dexterity in work is due to envy, to a jealous determination to outstrip our neighbours, to what Mallock calls "the desire for inequality." Now this spirit of rivalry, says Koheleth, is a mistake; it is vanity and vexation of spirit. The part of wisdom is to take life easily. The very sluggard, who folds his hands together and does nothing, has as much as he requires to eat: [the phrase rendered in our version, eats his flesh, should have been translated, eats his meat—that is, has enough to eat.] Better, says Koheleth, is a handful of peace, than two handfuls of labour accompanied by vexation of spirit; or, as our English proverb puts it, "A bird in the hand is worth two in the bush."

I need hardly point out that there is truth in this doctrine, but that it must not be pushed too far. The desire for inequality, as Mallock most clearly shows, is the source of all progress in art, science, and civilisation. Men would not work hard, they would not acquire "dexterity," except for the sake of getting on; and to get on means, to get above one's neighbours. But nevertheless, the desire for inequality requires to be held carefully under restraint, or else it may hurry a man on to his ruin. "Vaulting ambition doth o'erleap itself." The rash speculator, for example, in his over-eagerness for wealth, loses everything, and comes in the end to wish himself in the position of the man he used to despise—the man who was content with small profits or with a low rate of interest, and who is now enjoying his competence in peace. As Browning quaintly puts it—

> "That low man, adding one to one, his hundred's soon hit;
> This high man, aiming at a million, misses an unit."

Very often, Koheleth goes on to observe, the desire to outvie his neighbours is to be found in a man who is altogether alone in the world, who has neither child nor brother nor any near relation. He "bereaves his soul of good"—that is, he denies himself the enjoyment of his possessions—merely for the sake of accumulating and increasing them. It never occurs to him to ask, For whom am I labouring and hoarding? Such a man's life surely is vanity, or, as we should say, a mistake.

In contrast to the career of selfish isolation, of which he has just been speaking, Koheleth now describes the advantages of sympathetic co-operation with one's fellow-men. We should not, he says, strive *against* one another, each for his own good; we should strive *with* one another, each for the good of the whole. In any business undertaking, two are better than one; they will make more than double out of it. Co-operation is, therefore, preferable to competition. This doctrine he proceeds to enforce by five illustrations. First, he says, if two persons are travelling together, and one of them falls or meets with an accident, the other will be able to assist him; but the lonely traveller may perish for want of help. Secondly, if two sleep together they are warm. In the East, the heat of the day makes people peculiarly susceptible to the chills of night. And there are no glass windows in the houses; there are only lattices, which are intended to let in the light by day, but which also, of course, let in the cold by night. People sleep upon mats laid on the floor, and have usually no other covering than their outer garments. It is, therefore, considered disagreeable to sleep alone. There is a curious passage in the 'Mishna,' where the luxury of a bedfellow is forbidden, to those who have made a vow that they will derive no benefit from their neighbours. Thirdly, two persons will often be able to make an effectual resistance against thieves or banditti, when one would have no chance. Fourthly, a threefold cord cannot be broken; it is much more than three times as strong as each of the separate strands. The force of the fifth illustration, which begins in verse 13, will be enhanced if you remember, that formerly old age was much more reverenced, and youth much more despised, than is the case to-day. In the olden time, you see, books were scarce; information was communicated mostly by word of mouth; and the aged, who had had intercourse with the wise men of previous generations, were the depositories of all knowledge. But notwithstanding the oriental respect for age, Koheleth says, more fortunate is a poor youth who has been prudent enough to make friends, than an old and foolish king who knoweth not to be admonished [the marginal reading]—that is, who has lived such an isolated life, that no one ever cared to give him counsel or advice. The youth may have been thrown into prison by the king, but his popularity may lead to a revolution in his favour, and then all the world will flock to his standard. Verses 15 and 16 literally translated would be, "I see all the living, that walk under the sun, associating [not with the second child, but] with the youth who succeeds (*i.e.*, to the throne). There is no end to the people over whom he rules."

This is a pretty picture, a wonderful picture indeed, for a cynic like Koheleth to have drawn. But the old melancholy returns. "Those that come after the new king will not rejoice in him." His winning manners have taken him from the prison to the throne, and secured for him an almost universal dominion; but he will die, and be forgotten. So that *his* life also is vanity and vexation of spirit. Amiability, sociableness, sympathy, co-operation, all tend to improve life; but the life is no sooner improved than it is over. The game seems hardly worth the candle.

However, life must be lived; and it now occurs to Koheleth that we may perhaps find some help in religious observances. He has already pointed out to us how we are hemmed in on all sides by limitations and restrictions. It must evidently be important what attitude we assume towards the Power which thus checks and thwarts us. Take care, he says, how you go into the house of God, how you perform your sacrifices and prayers and vows. Koheleth teaches us, as wise men have always taught, that obedience is better than sacrifice. Our translation, "Be more ready to hear than to give the sacrifice of fools, for they consider not that they do evil," is misleading. The literal translation of the Hebrew would be,—It is nearer to obey than to offer the sacrifice of the disobedient, as they who obey know not to do evil—that is, it is a nearer way to God to obey His laws, than to offer sacrifices in atonement for disobedience. Those who obey have not done evil, and therefore require no such palliatives. In regard to prayer, Koheleth says, God is in heaven, and thou upon earth; therefore let thy words be few. Just as a multitude of persons and things, crowded confusedly together, constitute a dream, so a multitude of words constitute—nonsense.

Koheleth next speaks of vows. The practice of making vows without keeping them, without having any intention of keeping them, has been very common all the world over. Erasmus tells a story of a sailor who, during a storm at sea, was heard bawling out a promise to St Christopher of Paris, that if the saint would rescue him from drowning, he should be presented in return with a wax taper as big as his own statue. "Mind what you are about," said an acquaintance who overheard him; "you will never be able to pay for it." "Hold your tongue," said the man, speaking softly so that St Christopher should not hear him; "do you think I'm in earnest? If I once get my foot on dry ground, catch me giving him so much as a tallow candle." This story is only an extreme illustration of a belief that is common enough—the belief, viz., that the saints, that

God Himself, can be hoodwinked by religious observances which are unmeaning and dishonest. The Jews were especially given, under the influence of religious excitement, to make vows that they would do, or not do, certain things. They would dedicate their children to the service of the Temple, or their cattle to be offered up in sacrifice, or their lands to be devoted to purposes exclusively religious; or they would solemnly bind themselves to abstain from certain practices—as, for example, the drinking of wine. But when the excitement had passed away, they would very commonly try and shirk the promises which they had too rashly given. Such conduct Koheleth sternly condemns. If you have vowed a vow, he says, fulfil it; or else it would have been better never to have vowed at all. Inconstancy is the characteristic of fools! [Our translation, "He hath no pleasure in fools," is entirely wrong. The literal translation would be,—Fools have no steadfast will.] Therefore don't tell a lie about your vow. Do not let your mouth hurry you into sin. Don't tell the priest [so the word angel should, I think, have been rendered]—don't tell the priest it is a mistake, and that you never vowed so much. Instead of securing a blessing by this kind of vow, you will only obtain punishment. Such idle talk of dreaming fools is not worship, it is vanity, mere vapour.—But, adds Koheleth, fear thou God.

This advice in regard to worship, coming from a sceptic and a pessimist, is particularly striking. Though he has no faith in a future life, though he thinks that our present existence is contemptible and scarcely worth having, though he recommends us to give ourselves up to enjoyment, as being the highest good which this poor world can offer, yet he still clings in a way to the idea of righteousness. You are aware, of course, that the Jews—that is to say, the noblest and the best amongst them—had conceived a passionate enthusiasm for righteousness, an enthusiasm that has never been excelled and has rarely been equalled.[1] Koheleth had heard about righteousness at his mother's knee and at the Temple services, in the bright days of childhood before he left his home to indulge in the gaiety and study the philosophy of Alexandria. From the influence of these early impressions he never completely shook himself free.

[1] See my 'Defects of Modern Christianity, and other Sermons,' p. 193.

"You may break, you may shatter, the vase, if you will,
But the scent of the roses will hang round it still."

And so, here, we find Koheleth very much in earnest in his protestations against cant. There is one thing he tells us of which we may be very sure; dishonest simulation of religion is useless—worse than useless. Obedience is a nearer way to God than sacrifice. It is no good committing sins, and then trying to bribe the Almighty to forget them. We must not commit them, if we are to win His favour. Again, the value of prayer depends, not on its length, but on its sincerity. If our prayers are long, our thoughts will wander; and if our thoughts wander, our words will be meaningless; and such words addressed to God are nothing short of blasphemy. Remember, he says, that God is in heaven, and thou upon earth; therefore let thy words be few. Speak only out of the fulness of your heart. Speak only what you feel you must. Again, when suffering from terrible sickness, or threatened by some horrible calamity, you may have vowed that should the sickness be removed, or the calamity averted, you will thereafter live a better life. Woe be to you, says Koheleth, if you disregard your vow! God is not to be trifled with. He cannot be deluded into mistaking for worship what is mere idle talk.

But the majority of men seem always to have thought that He can. It is more than two thousand years since Koheleth sat down to write his little book; but we find them still falling into the same mistake. Men still take liberties with God, which they would never think of taking with a king; they try to cajole the Almighty, as they would never dream of attempting to cajole their fellow-men. They seem to look upon religion as a system of juggling, by which the penalties of vice are to be converted into the rewards of virtue. They imagine that by certain religious performances they will succeed in persuading the Deity they are good, when they know, and most of their acquaintances know, that they are not. There is no sadder sight, methinks, upon which the heavenly Father has to gaze, than an assemblage of seeming worshippers, many of whom, though drawing near to Him with their lips and in their attitude, are nevertheless in their heart and life far from Him—farther from Him than those who never pretend to worship. Now, however ignorant we may feel ourselves in regard to the nature of God,—Koheleth did not know much, and being an honest man, did not profess to know much,—however ignorant we may feel ourselves, we may at any rate be certain that the Creator of man can never be his dupe, and that there is no sin, at once more heinous and more foolish, than the attempt to impose upon the Almighty. Therefore let us listen, you and I, to the wise words of Koheleth, when he says, "Fear thou God."

Ecclesiastes.

V.

CHAPTERS V. 8—VII. 18.

WE left Koheleth in the act of exhorting us to fear God. The fear of God, of course, implies a belief in the divine superintendence of human affairs. This belief Koheleth now proceeds to justify.

Do not be alarmed, he says (v. 8) [such is the meaning of the words rendered "marvel not" in our version]—do not be alarmed when you see the injustice of oppressors. There are limits beyond which this injustice cannot go. The last half of verse 8, and the whole of verse 9, are entirely wrong in our version. Instead of "He that is higher than the highest regardeth; and there be higher than they. Moreover the profit of the earth is for all; and the king himself is served by the field:" instead of this we should read, There is superior watching superior, and superiors again over them—that is to say, each magistrate is held in check by some higher official; and there is one advantage which the common people have—there is one thing in their favour—viz., that this law of subjection extends to all, even to the king, who is dependent upon the industry of his people in the field. He cannot transgress against his subjects with impunity. And it is God, Koheleth intimates, who is the author of this system of restriction and punishment.

Again, the divine government may be seen, he says, in the law of compensation. Pleasure does not increase, but on the contrary rather diminishes, with the increase of wealth. The lover of money is not satisfied with accumulating and multiplying. Money is but vanity—mere vapour. As a man's riches increase, they are increased that eat them; for the number of his retainers must be augmented. The rich man has little to do but to watch others devouring his wealth. He is often kept awake by anxieties that arise out of his very abundance; but the poor man can always sleep, even though he has not enough to eat. This opinion of Koheleth's has often and often been corroborated. "Do you think," said Pheraules—a wealthy Persian of whom we read in Xenophon—"do you think I live with more pleasure the more I possess? By my abundance I gain merely this,—that I have to guard more and to distribute more. A great many domestics now demand of me their food, their drink, and their clothes. Some too are in want of physicians. And they are always bringing me bad news. One comes and tells me that my sheep have been torn by wolves; another that my oxen have been killed by falling over a precipice, and so on. Hence I seem to myself," said Pheraules, "in possessing abundance, to have more afflictions than when I was very poor."

Koheleth now returns to a thought on which he has before dwelt. The excessive desire for wealth often overreaches itself, and ends in poverty. "I have seen riches kept for the owners thereof to their hurt"—that is, badly kept as regards the *next* owners, never coming to the rightful heirs. The riches perish by evil travail—lost in some unlucky speculation; and the *quondam* millionaire becomes a beggar. As he came naked from the womb of the earth, so will he return thither, leaving no inheritance behind him for his son. It would have been bad enough had this been his only trouble. It would have been bad enough to discover, when he came to die, that he had but laboured for the wind, and that he must depart destitute as he had come. Even this would have been a sore evil. But his life has been miserable all through. He "eateth all his days in darkness;" he is anxious, sorrowful, vexed.

Koheleth now returns to his old position—that to eat and drink and enjoy one's self is the true end of life. But he points out that the faculty of enjoyment is not to be acquired by effort. Some have it; some have it not: it is the gift of God, or, as we should say, constitutional. The man who has been endowed with this faculty, forgets the transitoriness of life. God answereth him in the joy of his heart; his joy corresponds to God's; he lives in a state of divine tranquillity.

Our author then goes on to describe the misery of those who lack the faculty of enjoyment. I have seen, he says—and it is no uncommon sight—I have seen a man in the possession of wealth and honour, whose soul lacketh nothing of all that it desireth, but God hath not given him the power to enjoy it ["to eat thereof"]. He has not, it may be, any child to whom he can bequeath his possessions, but some stranger inherits them, and enjoys them as he did not. But even if he had a hundred children, even if he lived to a good old age, even if the grave were not awaiting him [this seems to be the meaning of the phrase, " have no burial "],—even then, unless his soul had been filled with good, that is to say unless he had had this faculty of enjoyment—a still-born child is better off than he. It cometh as nothingness; it goeth into darkness; its very memory is covered with darkness; it has known nothing of the sorrowful life which is lived under the sun. It hath more rest than he. Even if he were to live a thousand years twice told, in his accustomed state of unrestful joylessness, he must at last go to the same place, to the silent oblivion of the tomb. His miserable life cannot save him from the misery of death.

And now the gloom of our author deepens once again. He seems to forget what he has just admitted, that some men do manage to extract enjoyment out of life. He asserts (vi. 7) that no one ever does. "The labour of man is for his mouth,"—that is, for enjoyment; but he is never satisfied. His very wishes give him not his wish. In this respect the wise man is no better off than the fool, the obscure man is not more fortunate than the prince. [The man "who knoweth how to walk before the living," is the man of high birth and position, who lives before the eyes of the public.] You will notice the cynical irony of the idea, that the obscure man is not more fortunate than the prince! He has shown us that wealth and position very often bring with them additional anxiety, and now he implies that even obscurity and poverty have cares and troubles of their own. We shall be miserable if we are rich, and we shall be miserable even if we are poor. Better is the sight of the eyes than the wandering of desire; but even this, even the sight of the eyes, is vanity. He means to say, it is better to enjoy what we actually possess, than to spend our time in trying to get something beyond our reach. As Æsop put it in his fable, a small piece of meat, which the dog had in his mouth, was better than the large reflection for which he lost it. But even what we have, if judged by the test of pleasure, is vanity. We do not enjoy it. Pleasure itself does not please us. The very substance is after all but a shadow. The fact is, says Koheleth, returning to a former thought, everything has been predetermined for us; we are hemmed in by limits and fatalities to which we can but submit. It is useless trying to contend with One mightier than ourselves. The more we talk about it, the more sensible we become of our helplessness. [This is the meaning of what is rendered in our version—" many things increase vanity." It should be, many *words* increase vanity—that is, make us more conscious of it.] All our attempts to solve the mystery of existence are fruitless. We cannot tell what is really good for us; we know not whether there is anything that would actually make us happy during the numbered days of our vain life. That life passes away swiftly like a shadow. And what will come after it, who can say?

But fruitless as all such inquiries seem to be, Koheleth still pursues them. The heart-questionings of a thinker will not be silenced. He now takes a new departure. He inquires whether happiness is to be found in a life of social respectability or popularity. In chapter vii. and the first part of chapter viii., he gives us some of the maxims by which such a life would be guided. The thoughts are very loosely connected, but the underlying idea is this,—the popular man, the successful man, the man whom society delights to honour, is always characterised by prudence, discretion, moderation, self-control, and by a certain *savoir faire*—an instinct which teaches him what to do, and when to do nothing.

A good name, he begins, is more valuable than precious ointment—more valuable, that is to say, than the crowning luxury of oriental life. For the man who has acquired such a name, even death has lost much of its horror. The day on which he dies is happier than that on which he was born. *Then* it was doubtful how he would deal with life, and how life would deal with him; doubtful whether his birth were not a deplorable calamity. But *now*, dying in the possession of a good name, he has proved himself a hero, a victor, to whom life has not been vouchsafed in vain.

The uncertainty which surrounds an infant's future, has been keenly felt by others besides Koheleth. For example, Herodotus mentions a Thracian tribe, which always celebrated the birth of a child by lamentation and mourning. There is a story in the 'Midrash' that illustrates the same idea. Two vessels once met at the harbour-bar. Silence prevailed on the one which was returning from its voyage, mirth on the one which was just about to start. At this sight, a wise man exclaimed, What a perverted world! Mirth should be found on the vessel which has returned in safety, silence on that which has yet to encounter the perils of the sea. And just so, added the wise man, the true occasion for joy is, not the beginning of a human career, but its end, when a man enters with a good report into the haven of rest.

It is better, says Koheleth again, to go to the house of mourning than to the house of feasting. I have told you before that, in the East, it is a point of etiquette to pay formal visits of condolence. The man, therefore, who goes in for social respectability, must be scrupulous in discharging this obligation. Koheleth points out that it is a useful, as well as a respectable, practice. Death, he says, is the end of all, and the sight of it will lead us to reflect. It is a mistake to be always trying to avoid sorrow. There is a pleasure in melancholy, and a sweetness in woe. Thoughtful sadness, sadness with reflection, is better than unthinking laughter. The calamities which sadden the expression of the countenance, may develop the affections of the heart. The wise man, therefore, loves to linger in the house of mourning. He who feels at home only in the midst of gaiety is, says Koheleth, a fool.

The wise man too is ready to receive instruction, not only from the silent teaching of the dead, but also from the advice of the living, if they are wiser than himself. There is more melody in the censure of a wise man than in the song of a fool. In fact, the merriment of fools is always vanity; it is like the crackling of thorns under a pot. The fuel generally used in the East is charcoal, which burns slowly. In a fit of impatience, people would be inclined to employ dried thorns. But these, though they made a great noise, produced hardly any effect. They were all sputter and no heat. Similarly, in a fool's song there is nothing but sound; while wise advice may be productive of permanent good.

He mentions the case of bribery and corruption, as an instance in which censure would be salutary. [The word rendered "gift" in verse 7 should be rather, I think, extortion or corruption.] Even a wise man, he says, becomes infatuated by corrupt practices. How sadly the truth of this maxim was proved in the history of Lord Bacon, whom Pope describes as "the wisest, brightest, meanest of mankind"! It is illustrated, too, in the mischievous system of place-hunting which prevails in America, the evils of which have been so graphically described in 'Democracy.' But it is in the East that bribery has been carried to the greatest lengths, and been productive of the greatest misery. Well then, says Koheleth, since even wise men become infatuated by corrupt practices, the rebuke which puts a stop to them must be good. It may be distasteful, but nevertheless it is beneficial. Better is the end of it than the beginning. [Instead of " Better is the end of a thing," read,—Better is the end of a word—that is, of the reproof.] The censure should therefore be received with patience, instead of being resented in pride. Do not give way, he says, to your first hasty impulse of anger. It is not unnatural that you should feel inclined to resent the interference; but, if you are wise, you will get the better of this feeling. Anger resteth in the bosom of fools. It is the part of a wise man, when he receives good advice, not to abuse the counsellor, but to follow the counsel. And even if he do not follow it, receiving it gracefully will tend to increase his popularity.

In verse 10 he proceeds to point out that " the wise man "—the prudent man of the world whose portrait he is sketching for us, the man who manages to win the liking and esteem of his fellows—is distinguished by a cheerful, easy-going, happy temperament. He is not one of those disagreeable persons, who are always inquiring why the former days were better than these, who are perpetually sighing for the good old times. Instead of longing for the past, he makes the best of the present. Our version here puts a cynical remark into Koheleth's mouth, which he did not utter. He does not say, "Wisdom is good with an inheritance—all very well for persons of property." He says, "Wisdom is as good as an inheritance, and even better." There is a profit or advantage in possessing it, over and above that which can be derived from money; for wisdom giveth life to them that have it—that is, it *enliveneth* them, enables them to be cheerful, hopeful, and glad. The word translated defence means primarily shadow. In the scorching climate of the East, shade often affords a shelter against heat which, without it, might be quite fatal. Hence the word came, secondarily, to mean protection or defence. In the East, too, heat is often regarded as typifying the ills of life. Koheleth means to say, therefore, wisdom is a shelter or defence from calamity, inasmuch as it makes men cheerful, and cheerfulness is the best possible protection against the ills that flesh is heir to. A merry heart doeth good like a medicine.

> "It bars a thousand harms and lengthens life."

The man who possesses a sanguine temperament will quickly recover from a shock that might otherwise have driven him mad. And a cheerful disposition is particularly useful to those who would stand well in the estimation of their fellows. "It is pleasant," says George Eliot, "to see some men turn round—pleasant as a sudden rush of warm air in winter, or a flash of firelight in the chill dusk." Men thus gifted are naturally very welcome in society.

In verses 13 and 14, Koheleth points out how it is that wisdom tends to develop cheerfulness. It does this by showing us the uselessness of kicking against the pricks. The times may be crooked; but God has made them so, and we cannot straighten them. We should take them as they come, and make the best of them. By grumbling at the established order of things, we do not change it; we only injure ourselves.[1] In the day of prosperity therefore, he says, enjoy your prosperity; and in the day of adversity, bethink you that it has not come by accident—it has been sent by God for a purpose.

[1] See sermons on "True and False Discontent," in my 'Inspiration, and other Sermons.'

He interweaves the joy and sorrow of human life in the way He does, so that we may never be able to foresee what is awaiting us in the future. Since then God has a definite purpose in our adverse circumstances, it is not to be expected He will change them for any fretting or fuming on our part. The best thing for us to do is to make His pleasure ours; and, as we cannot get what we like, to school ourselves into liking what we get.

> " To will what God doth will, that is the only science
> Which gives us any rest."

Koheleth now propounds another maxim of worldly policy—a maxim in which we see him at his worst. During the days of my vanity, he begins, during my unsatisfactory life, I have observed the righteous man die prematurely, notwithstanding his righteousness, and the wicked man live to a good old age, notwithstanding his wickedness. Prosperity and adversity seem to come to men, not in accordance with their merit or demerit, but at the bidding of the divine caprice. A prudent man of the world, therefore, will not trouble himself too much about righteousness. He cannot be quite sure that it will pay; though a certain amount of it is likely to help him on. And what is true of righteousness is true of wisdom. Too much wisdom will keep him back. Why shouldst thou [not "destroy thyself?" as our version reads]—why shouldst thou isolate thyself? People won't like you if you're too good; they will call you a fanatic. They won't like you if you're too wise; they will call you a prig. Therefore be not overmuch righteous, neither make thyself overwise. At the same time, you must take care to avoid the opposite extreme. Don't be overmuch wicked. Don't be a fool. Over-indulgence in certain kinds of sin would be sure to bring you to an untimely grave. The best plan, says Koheleth, is to go in for both —for moderate righteousness and for moderate wickedness. Such is the practice of the God-fearing man—that is, of the man who is God-fearing in the eyes of society, who is religious according to the fashionable standard of religiousness. In other words, we shall be to all intents and purposes sufficiently righteous, if we are only moderately wicked. Poor Koheleth, in his present mood, has fallen into deep moral degradation. The idea of righteousness, in which he was brought up, has been supplanted by the notion of expediency. Policy has taken the place of duty. The doctrine he is now preaching is precisely the doctrine of Lucifer, in Longfellow's "Golden Legend"—

> "We must look at the Decalogue in the light
> Of an ancient statute, that was meant
> For a mild and general application,
> To be understood with the Reservation,
> That, in certain instances, the Right
> Must yield to the expedient."

There are too many among us, I am afraid, who are devoted followers of Lucifer. We believe, above all things, in expediency. The vices which society condemns we look upon with a pious horror; but we see no harm in the vices which society approves. For instance :—we *ought* to set ourselves studiously against the prevalent practice of scandal and mischief-making. But we do not. People would be angry with us if we tacitly or openly rebuked them, if we refused to join them in their favourite recreation. And therefore we repeat to ourselves the comforting advice of Koheleth,—Be not righteous overmuch. Why shouldst thou isolate thyself? Why make thyself unpopular for the sake of a paltry peccadillo? Everything is a peccadillo nowadays, *if it be only condemned by God.* Such condemnation counts for nothing, in comparison with the condemnation of society. When the laws of God come into collision with the laws of society, it is generally the latter that prevail. Men who will brave the divine anger with the greatest possible composure, are thrown into despair by the disapproval of their neighbours and acquaintances. Sirs! let us shake ourselves free from this unwholesome fear of man. Let us dare to do our duty, even though we are frowned upon for our pains. In the long-run the policy of expediency, which Koheleth here calls wisdom, will turn out to be but folly. We shall see plainly enough in the next life, if not in this,

> "That because right is right, to do the right
> Were wisdom, in the scorn of consequence."

Ecclesiastes.

VI.

CHAPTERS VII. 19—VIII. 15.

THE successful man of the world, Koheleth has told us, will always be careful to conform to the social standard, in matters of morality and religion. He will see to it that he is neither better, nor worse, than society requires. Nothing will help us on in life, he says, more than this judicious combination of moderate righteousness with moderate wickedness. In wisdom (verse 19)—that is, in this practical sagacity— there lies greater strength than in an armed force. ["Ten armed men" means, of course, an indefinite number.]

Then, as if his conscience rather smote him for the immoral morality he has been preaching, he adds,—Righteousness, in the strict sense, is unattainable; there is not upon earth a just man, that doeth good and sinneth not. It is useless for us, therefore, to trouble about an unattainable ideal. If we are good enough to pass muster with our neighbours, we shall do.

It is also the part of wisdom—of that practical wisdom which, as he tells us, makes a man cheerful—not to mind what people say of us. If we indulge our curiosity in this matter, we shall find our very servants abusing us; and we need not be surprised at it, he intimates, for "thou thyself likewise hast cursed (or abused) others." It is human nature. He means to say, that in spite of our attempt to conform to the common social standard, we need not expect to please everybody. Men must amuse themselves; and there is no amusement which they find so enjoyable, as the discovery and discussion of their neighbours' defects. "Could we," says Lord Bacon, "procure some magic glass, in which to view the animosity and malice directed against us, it would be better for us to break it directly than to use it." We shall never have any peace if we attend to tittle-tattle. Let us therefore, says Koheleth, pursue our course unmoved.

In verse 23 he tells us that he had himself proved, by experience, the truth and value of the preceding maxims. He seems to have had a suspicion, however, all the time, that this view of life was a low one. He intimates that he had tried for a better, but failed to reach it. "I said I will be wise, but it was far from me." There was, he admits, or there conceivably might be, a higher wisdom which he had not acquired. There was much, he felt, which he did not at all understand. "Far remaineth" [so verse 24 should read]—" far remaineth what was far, and deep remaineth what was deep." After all his thinking, he knew he had not completely fathomed the mystery of life, he had not completely solved the problem of existence. It is beyond him, he must give up all thoughts of it. In lieu of such a perfect theory or complete philosophy, he returns again to the lower wisdom of commonsense—the wisdom which contents itself with partial explanations and suggestive maxims, available for our guidance in everyday life.

From this lower standpoint he now sets himself to inquire into the origin of evil. I applied my mind, he says, to discover the cause of wickedness and vice and mad folly. He finds it, as he thinks, in woman. I found woman, he says, more bitter than death. She is a net; her heart is a snare; her hands are chains. He who finds favour in the sight of God shall escape from her; but the sinner shall become her prey. Look you, this is my experience. One man among a thousand human beings I have found, one who was genuine and true, and who really deserved the name of man; but a genuine woman have I not found. This remark is no hasty generalisation. I have conducted my inquiries most carefully, picking out my specimens one by one, so as to avoid the possibility of mistake. God made man upright, but they became corrupted by wicked devices, especially by the devices of the female sex. Women, therefore, will be treated by the wise man with the contempt which they deserve.—I will return to this doctrine presently; but let us first finish Koheleth's description of the prudent man of the world.

Having pointed out, in chapter vii., how such a man conducts himself in social life, at the beginning of chapter viii. he tells us how he would behave himself in politics. He starts off with another eulogium on wisdom. There is nothing like wisdom, he begins, nothing like the practical wisdom, which enables a man to understand the *rationale* of life, which helps him, in cases of emergency, to comprehend the situation and to be master of it. Wisdom makes a man cheerful and illuminates his countenance, not only under the apparent tyranny of God, of which he has spoken before, but also under the actual tyranny of man.

The wise man adapts himself to the pressure of circumstances. He never, for example, attempts to carry on an unequal warfare with an all-powerful despot. Whatever be the king's commandment, he obeys. The words, "in regard to the oath of God," seem to refer to the practice, among Babylonian and Persian despots, of exacting an oath of loyalty from conquered races, each race being made to swear by the god it worshipped. The wise man bethinks him, that the prince who had power to exact a promise of obedience, will have power to punish disobedience; and therefore he obeys. In verse 3, the words rendered in our version, " Stand not in an evil thing," should be,—Resent not an evil, or angry, word. Be not hasty to go out of the king's sight; don't throw up your allegiance because he is angry. Resistance is fatal. He is practically omnipotent; no one dares to say unto him, what doest thou?—to ask him to justify or explain his conduct. Whoso keepeth the commandment " shall feel no evil word," *i.e.*, will not incur his anger.

And further, a wise man's heart discerneth

[not time and judgment, but] the time of judgment. If you would obey him, he would not be angry with you; or even if he were, a wise man would discern the time of judgment, would find comfort in looking forward to the day of retribution. Verse 6 should read, instead of "To every purpose there is time and judgment, therefore the misery of man is great upon him,"—instead of this it should be—To every purpose there is a time of judgment, *when* the misery of man is great upon him. That is, when the sufferings of the subjects become intolerable, there will be a revolution, and the actions of the tyrant will be revenged. The wise man knows that he cannot, single-handed, make a successful resistance; he will wait till the times be ripe. He will comfort himself with the assurance, that beyond a certain point tyranny cannot go. When it reaches that point there will be a reaction against it; despotism will be "tempered by assassination." The tyrant exercises his tyranny unrestrainedly, for he knoweth not that which shall be; and who can tell him when it shall be? He does not foresee the dire fate that is in store for him; or, at any rate, he never expected it would come so soon. But the day of reckoning, the day of death, does come. Then no man has power to retain his spirit. There is no ruler [not power] in the day of death. The distinction between kings and subjects is then broken down. The tyrant himself becomes subject to the king of terrors. In the warfare against death there is no leave of absence; no cunning can save a man; not even his wickedness can avail him, though it would shrink from nothing by which escape might be secured.—In all this, says Koheleth, I am speaking from personal observation, having set myself diligently to examine into all the transactions of men.

I must confess however, he adds, that sometimes the tyrant tyrannises with impunity. There is a time when one ruleth over another [not to his own hurt, as our version puts it, but] to the other's hurt. Verse 10 is nonsense in our version. It should be,—I have seen the wicked honourably buried, and come to life again, as it were, in his wicked children; and on the other hand, I have seen the righteous turned out of the place of the holy (that is to say excommunicated) and treated with contumely while they lived, and entirely forgotten when they died. So that the idea of inevitable retribution, on which he had just been insisting, he now sees to be but vanity. There is no such thing. Sentence against an evil deed is not executed speedily; sometimes it is not executed at all. The sinner keeps on doing evil ["does it a hundred times"], and yet lives to a good old age. It is because they perceive this, that the hearts of the sons of men are fully set in them to do evil. There seems nothing to hinder them. Verse 12 in our version puts a pious sentiment into the mouth of Koheleth, which he did not utter. The word "know" should have been translated in the past tense; it is in contrast with the present tense of verse 14. He does not say, "I know that it will be well with them that fear God," but,—I knew: I used to believe it. The wicked, I once thought, would not prolong his days, but would pass away quickly like a shadow. That was my belief. But facts are stronger than creeds. There is a vanity which takes place on the earth, and which disproves my former conviction. There be just men, unto whom it happeneth according to the work of the wicked; and again, there be unjust men, unto whom it happeneth according to the work of the righteous. Good men are treated by Providence as if they were bad, and bad men are treated as if they were good.

Therefore, he says, this also is vanity. The scheme of life which he has just been sketching is found, like the others, to break down. A man may be prudent, moderate, self-controlled; he may do his best to conform to all the standards of society; he may act always on the most approved principles; and yet, both in civil and political life, come to grief. He may fail to win the social approbation and popularity which would have been the fitting reward of his labour. Circumstances over which he had, and could have, no control—such as the loss of his health or the loss of his money—may render all his efforts nugatory—

> "The best laid schemes o' mice and men
> Gang aft a-gley."

There is something in the world amiss, which not unfrequently upsets the most careful calculations, and makes us look like fools, when we have been all along priding ourselves on our wisdom. Koheleth finds himself driven back, therefore, to the conclusion, that there is no good in having any scheme of life at all. In this topsy-turvy world the chances are we shall do best by not trying to do well. I commended mirth, he says; there is nothing better for a man under the sun than to eat, drink, and be merry; there is nothing better for a man than the enjoyment which [not "abides with him in his labour," but which] follows him in his labour. True enjoyment comes of its own accord. We shall probably miss it altogether, if we set ourselves systematically to seek it.—You will observe, he bids us discard the career of the man of the world, not because he is dissatisfied with any of the maxims which he has laid down for our guidance in that *rôle*, but because it is not in maxims to command success. He perceives that, however consistently we may act upon the maxims, we may still, by some unlucky *contretemps*, be done out of our reward. Of his maxims, as such, he still approves.

Now, from our modern point of view, the two most important doctrines which he has enunciated, in this connection, are the doctrine of righteousness, of which I have already spoken, and the doctrine of women, on which I must now beg leave to say a word.

Woman, he thinks, is *par excellence* the great cause of evil. By her fatal gift of beauty she often lures men to a doom more bitter than death; and at the best she has but a shallow, unbalanced nature, capable of doing much mischief, but incapable of doing any good. In these notions Koheleth does not stand alone. Adam set the example of depreciating the sex, when he declared that he would have been a better man but for the influence of his wife. And his example was followed, almost without exception, century after century, millennium after millennium. There are one or two curious facts that prove the prevalence of Koheleth's notions among the Jews. Women were considered so frivolous and untrustworthy, that their evidence was never accepted in a court of justice. The rabbis maintained that this was the intention of the Mosaic law, which, when referring to witnesses, always used the masculine, and never the feminine, gender. In Zechariah (v. 8) you will notice, the prophet finds in woman an emblem or type of wickedness. And to this day, a recognised part of the morning thanksgiving, offered up by every male Jew, is the following: "Blessed be Thou, O Lord God, King of the universe, that Thou hast not created me a woman." Similar opinions prevailed among Greek thinkers—one of whom, for example, said, "The natural home of folly is a woman's heart;" and another, "Where women are, there is every evil." The Arabians have a proverb to the effect, that when woman was created the devil was delighted, and said to her, "Thou shalt be my arrow, with which I will shoot and not miss." Mohammed is commonly supposed to have maintained that women, as such, would be excluded from heaven. This is a popular error. He did however assert that the majority of them would, in point of fact, be found in hell. And the same, or similar, views we find prevailing even amongst the Christian fathers. Chrysostom tells us that when the devil took from Job all he had, he was careful to leave his wife, as he knew she would assist him in the task of leading the saint from God. The depreciatory estimate of women used to be accepted almost as a truism, and was not unfrequently adopted by women themselves. It is a woman whom Euripides represents as saying, that one man is better than ten thousand of her own sex.

To many of us, I suppose, these sentiments will appear almost inexplicable. Surely, we say to ourselves, the women of whom such things were said, must have been very different from the women of the present day. And no doubt they were: different through no fault of their own, but by reason of the treatment to which they had been subjected. I know men now, who have such a poor opinion of the female intellect, that they never condescend to offer a lady anything but small-talk—generally *very* small talk. Let one of these gentlemen hold a conversation with the most brilliant woman living, and, to a fool like him, her intellect will appear but feeble. Now contempt for women—a contempt that included their moral, as well as their intellectual, nature—was at one time universal; and it inevitably had on them a deteriorating effect. Let men be dealt with for a hundred years, as women were for thousands; let them be taught to consider themselves mere drudges or toys,—and what do you suppose they would be worth at the end of it?

As soon as woman received fair-play, she proved herself not only equal to men, but superior; lacking, no doubt, some of his best qualities, but possessing others which more than compensate for the deficiency. It has become a proverb with us that "'tis the low man thinks the woman low." Generally speaking, a man's intellectual and moral worth, or worthlessness, may be very fairly tested by his respect, or want of respect, for women. Scarcely any one, in the present day, whose opinion deserves a moment's consideration—with the exception of one or two pessimists like Schopenhauer or

Hartmann—scarcely any one would agree with Koheleth. Instead of his arithmetical calculation about the thousand men and the thousand women, most persons would substitute Oliver Wendell Holmes'—that there are at least three saints among women for one among men.

Shakespeare's experience curiously enough, if we may judge by the 144th Sonnet, was very similar to Koheleth's:—

> "Two loves I have, of comfort and despair,
> Which, like two spirits, do suggest me still.
> The better angel is a man right fair,
> The worser spirit a woman coloured ill.
> To win me soon to hell my female evil
> Tempteth my better angel from my side;
> And would corrupt my saint to be a devil,
> Wooing his purity with her foul pride."

But this notwithstanding, Shakespeare knew that the best women were better than the best men. You cannot study his plays carefully, without perceiving that he had a mysterious veneration for the true womanly character—a veneration as for something higher and more divine than man's. In this view he is kept in countenance by Goethe, Petrarch, Dante, Raphael, Rousseau, Jean Paul Richter, and a host of others. Among our own countrymen there have been none abler in the present generation than Lord Beaconsfield and

John Stuart Mill, and none ever thought more highly of women. If you want proof of this, glance over Mill's 'Autobiography,' and read the dedication to 'Sybil.'

We are beginning, at last, to perceive the immense importance of the part which women have played in the culture and moral development of the race. It is they who inspire us with the holiest and the strongest moral impulses. There is nothing in the world so helpful to a man as the influence of a good woman, be she mother or sister, lover or friend or wife. I say there is nothing so helpful to a man as the influence of such a woman, if only he recognise and reverence her goodness. There is no inspiration like it. It will keep him true to himself and to God.

> "Trust in all things high
> Comes easy to him; and though he trip and fall,
> He shall not blind his soul with clay."

"What," asks George Eliot, "in the midst of the mighty drama of life, are girls and their blind visions? They are the yea or nay of that good for which men are enduring and fighting. In these delicate vessels is borne onward through the ages the treasure of human affection;" and with affection all that is purest, noblest, most divine. In the great hereafter, when human character has been perfected, it will be seen, I believe, that man's contribution to that result, compared with woman's, is but poor and insignificant.

Ecclesiastes.

VII.

CHAPTERS VIII. 16—X. 9.

AT the end of chapter viii. and the beginning of chapter ix., Koheleth points out that it is impossible for us to construct a satisfactory philosophy of life. He had devoted himself to the subject, he says, most diligently, taking rest neither by night nor day, and yet the result was failure. " The work of God "—or, as we say, the ways of Providence—cannot be fathomed. To the wisest man, labour as he may to understand it, the drift of the Maker is dark. We can never know why He does things. We can never foresee what He is going to do. Providence is arbitrary and inscrutable. It is for this reason that theories and schemes of life are altogether useless. In the moral world there is no reign of law to form a rational basis for our actions. For example, righteousness and wisdom avail us nothing. The righteous and the wise, no less than the unrighteous and the foolish, are in the hands of God, and He does with them what He likes. He treats them in an utterly inexplicable and unpredictable fashion. They know not, by the outward events of their life, whether they are the objects of His love or of His hatred. "All things are before them,"— that is, anything may happen to them. Happiness and misery come to them indiscriminately, in the same arbitrary manner as to other men. All things come alike to all; there is the same fate for the righteous and for the wicked. Those whose hearts have been mad with sin, can but die in the end; and from that fate the best of us cannot possibly escape.

Here he breaks off into a parenthetical description of the wretchedness of death. The living at any rate, he says, have hope. Times may be bad with them, but they can always look forward in imagination to better. This idea Koheleth very probably derived from the Greek legend of Pandora. She had been intrusted by the gods, you remember, with a box containing the various blessings which they wished to bestow upon the human race. She was forbidden to open it until she reached her destination; but overcome by curiosity, she lifted the lid prematurely, and all the blessings intended for mortals flew away, with the single exception of hope, which remained at the bottom of the box. Unhappy in all other respects, we are happy in our faculty of hope. But *even of this* death deprives us. A living dog, therefore —or as we should say, a living rat—is better than a dead lion. Dogs, of course, in the East were never treated as pets or companions. They were never allowed about the premises, but were banished to the desolate, outlying parts of the town or village; and there they lived on carrion. They were regarded with much the same disgust as we now feel for rats. The living, at any rate, he continues, know that they must die; and even to know this melancholy fact, is better than to be altogether destitute of consciousness like the dead. There is a certain greatness and grandeur in the very knowledge of our coming doom. But the dead know not anything; neither have they any [not "reward," but] compensation for this loss of knowledge. Their memory is gone. Their loves and their hatreds are over. Their zeal [not envy] has come to an end—that is to say, nothing can any longer excite or stimulate them. They take no interest in anything that is done under the sun.

Since, then, this miserable fate is in store for you, says Koheleth, and since it may overtake you at any moment, in spite of your best laid plans, enjoy life while you can; seize upon the pleasure that offers itself; eat and drink with a merry heart. God won't mind,—you need have no fear upon that score. God will accept these works of yours. He will be just as pleased with this mode of life, as with any other that you could adopt. The deeds of the pleasure-seeker are as likely to be followed by the outward signs of divine approval, as the deeds of the man who has gone in for religiousness or for wisdom. Let thy garments therefore be always white, and let thy head lack no ointment. White garments are of course particularly pleasant in a hot climate: but, from the expense of keeping them clean, it is the wealthy alone who wear them daily; others can only afford them on festive occasions. Both white garments and perfumes are regarded as symbols of prosperity and good cheer. All classes abstain from them on occasions of mourning. Koheleth's meaning, therefore, is—live always in luxury and festivity.

He adds, "with her whom thou lovest." I am sorry to say the Hebrew word does not necessarily mean wife. In chapter vii., you remember, his advice was to beware of women and to avoid them. But then he was speaking to would-be men of the world, who wished to live according to a fixed and rational plan. Here he is advising us to discard all such elaborate schemes of life, and to accept every happiness that offers itself, without stopping to inquire particularly into its wisdom or expediency. This, I apprehend, is the explanation of the apparent change in his views regarding women. The enjoyment of life, he adds, is "your portion"—that is, your destiny, your duty, your end. Therefore, whatever thy hand findeth to do, do it with thy might. Embrace eagerly every opportunity for gratification; for there is no work, nor device, nor knowledge, nor wisdom in the grave, whither thou goest. The only thing in this universe we can be sure about is pleasure. Therefore let us get pleasure while we may.

He has shown us already the uncertainty, and consequent uselessness, of piety. He has shown us that good men and bad men experience joy and sadness indiscriminately, and at last meet with the same fate of death. He now proceeds to point out (verse 11) the uselessness of "wisdom and skill," of what we should call ability. It is not, he says, the swift who win the race, nor the strong who gain the battle. Wisdom, intelligence, learning, will procure for a man neither favour nor money, scarcely even bread. Misfortunes come upon the most deserving, and they cannot be foreseen. Providence ensnares us in calamity, just as birds are entangled in a net. And, besides the thwarting of Providence, able men have to suffer from the ingratitude of their fellows. The world is slow to reward the ability to which it owes so much. Koheleth here relates a little anecdote in point. He tells us how a small and defenceless city was attacked by a powerful army. In addition to its immense superiority of numbers, this army had the advantage of occupying high ground, upon which citadels were planted, commanding the very heart of the town. In this desperate emergency "a poor man"—some unknown citizen—was clever enough to hit upon a stratagem by which the besiegers were put to flight. Yet no one remembered that same poor man. As far as reward went, he might as well have been a fool. Wisdom, says Koheleth, is no doubt, in itself and theoretically, a very good thing. As the story shows, it is "better than strength"—that is, stronger than mere brute force. But, generally speaking, no one will listen to the wise man if he happen to be poor. Verse 17 should read—instead of "The words of wise men are heard in quiet, more than the cry of him that ruleth among fools"—The quiet words of a wise man are listened to, when the shouting of a foolish ruler is disregarded. As in the story just related, the commands of the incompetent generals were superseded by the advice of a private citizen who possessed ability. Such wisdom, such ability, is better than weapons of war, more effective than the most imposing military preparations. Sometimes it does happen, Koheleth says, that the advice of a wise man is taken, in spite of his being poor. But one fool [not sinner] destroyeth much good. One fool will undo the work that it took many wise men to accomplish. Just as dead flies spoil the ointment of the perfumer, by imparting to it their own ill savour, so a little folly—one or two fools—will often lead the community to disregard the counsels of men who ought to be held in universal honour for their wisdom. Flies in a sultry climate are even greater nuisances than they are in ours. There is an Arabic proverb to the effect, "flies are nothing, yet they cause loathsomeness." Their resemblance, therefore, to fools is evident. The fool is a great power in the world, especially the conceited fool. His self-assurance is mistaken for knowledge; while the modesty of the wise man is thought to be ignorance. Over and over again in the history of the world, the fools of a nation have taken upon themselves to decry the wise men; and in such cases the popular sympathy has generally been with the fools.

However, though wisdom is thus often counteracted by folly, it is better to have it than to have it not. The mind of the wise man is at his right hand, but a fool's is at his left. To be on a man's right hand signifies to protect him, as in the Psalmist's phrase, "The Lord is on my right hand; I shall not be moved." A wise man's mind, Koheleth means, is of some use to him; a fool's is not. The fool, says Koheleth (verse 3), no sooner sets his foot in the street than he is bewildered; he is ignorant of the commonest roads in the very place where he has spent his life; and yet he says [not to every one, but] of every one he meets, that he is a fool. All men are fools but himself. "As you read the verse," says Mr Cox, "the unhappy wretch stands before you. You see him coming out of his house, he goes dawdling down the street, attracted from his path by the merest trifle, staring at familiar objects with eyes that have no recognition in them, and with pointed finger chuckles after every sober citizen he meets, There goes a fool." Just as a drunkard thinks every one drunk but himself, and a madman thinks every one mad, so a fool imagines the whole human race, with one solitary exception, to be altogether destitute of wisdom.

Koheleth now contrasts this self-assertiveness of fools with the yielding self-effacement of the wise man; and he illustrates the point by referring, again, to the importance and necessity of submitting to the king. If, he says—addressing himself more particularly to statesmen—if the spirit of the ruler rise up against thee, leave not thy place; if the sovereign is angry with you, don't resign your office in a pet. For yielding [not "pacifieth great offences," as in our version, but] prevents greater outrages. The Hebrew word for yielding, it is significant to notice, means literally healing. The sovereign will often displease us by his actions, and especially by the selection of his favourites; but for this we must be prepared. I have seen the fool, says Koheleth, occupying an exalted position, and the noble [not rich] living in degradation. I have seen servants—that is, those who should have been servants—riding upon horses as masters; and those who should have been masters proceeding, like servants, upon foot. To ride upon horseback was formerly considered a mark of distinction. Among the Parthians it was a privilege restricted to men of gentle birth. Maundrell relates that, in early days, the Europeans who visited Turkey were only allowed to ride upon asses or mules—an exception being made, however, in favour of the consuls of the great Powers. Still, says Koheleth, however unjust the monarch may be, it is useless, worse than useless, for us to offer him any resistance. In trying to destroy the despot, we shall only destroy ourselves. The truth of this he proceeds to exemplify, by several illustrations taken from common life. He who digs a pit is very likely to fall into it. Here, of course, the allusion is to the pit dug by the huntsman. It was covered over lightly with foliage, so that when an animal stepped on to it, attracted by some dainty morsel, the covering gave way and the animal fell in—unless by some accident the huntsman had fallen in first. This he was very apt to do, if he dug many pits, and did not carefully remember their locality. In the same way, says Koheleth, our treachery to the sovereign, if he find it out, may prove our ruin. Again, he who breaks down a wall is very likely to be bitten by serpents. These creatures are fond of building their nests in quiet nooks and crannies. In countries where serpents abound, pulling down a wall is therefore a dangerous amusement. No less dangerous, says Koheleth, is the attempt to dethrone a tyrant. In the effort, we shall break up the nests of the human reptiles, the venomous hangers-on, that abound in every court. It will be to their advantage to resist us, and we shall only be bitten for our pains. Again, he who removeth stones shall be hurt therewith; and he that cleaveth wood shall be endangered thereby. Here the reference is to the pulling down of a building, for which in those days they had very imperfect appliances. The danger of the employment was therefore much greater than at present. No less dangerous is it, says Koheleth, to attempt subverting the structure of a despotic government. Even if we succeed in overthrowing it, we may be injuriously affected by its ruin.

Before I conclude, just allow me to call your attention again to Koheleth's argument, contained in the beginning of chapter ix. More distinctly than he has yet done, he here bases his advocacy of a life of pleasure upon the grounds—first, that our existence practically ends with death; and secondly, that amid the uncertainties which surround us, present enjoyment is the only thing of which we can really make sure. In the grave, whither we are going, there is neither work, nor device, nor knowledge, nor wisdom. Everything we can ever hope to obtain must therefore come to us within the compass of our earthly life. That is short enough at the best; and at the worst—why, at any moment it may come to an end. And, besides death, there is a whole host of unforeseen calamities, that may suddenly arise, and spoil for us the remainder of our existence. If we live according to an elaborate scheme, denying ourselves pleasure in the present, in order that we may reap some great reward by-and-by, all our plans may be suddenly nullified by some unexpected interference on the part of God. The wisest course for us therefore, says Koheleth, is to live, not for the future, but in the present; to give up the attempt to solve the problem of existence or to formulate an elaborate scheme of life, and to devote ourselves to those enjoyments which lie immediately within our reach. The present moment is ours; let us see to it, therefore, that it be a moment of pleasure.

A poor philosophy is this of Koheleth's; but it seems to me the only philosophy possible for any one who, like Koheleth, disbelieves in immortality. It may strike you as strange that among the various aims in life which Koheleth discusses, he never mentions character. And yet it would have been stranger if he had. For what is the good of character to a being who may at any moment be turned into clay? Pleasure is always pleasurable, more or less; but the struggle for perfection is painful, and, in this life at any rate, unsuccessful. To sacrifice pleasure for character then, *apart from immortality*, would be to give up the possible for the impossible, the certain for the uncertain, the real for the chimerical, the valuable for the worthless. If the wages of virtue be dust, you can never prove its reasonableness. If goodness be doomed to annihilation, it loses all, or nearly all, its charm. Convince me that I must be extinguished some day, and that I may be extinguished any day, and I too should agree with Koheleth, that my only rational course was to enjoy to the utmost the few moments that might be vouchsafed to me. Let me feel, on the other hand, that I carry latent within me "the power of an endless life," and that some day in the great hereafter it is possible I may find myself "perfect even as God is perfect," then I can despise pleasure; I can see beauty in pain; I can keep under my body and bring it into subjection; I can resist "even unto blood" in my striving against sin; I can gather up all the energies of my being and consecrate them to righteousness and to God with enthusiastic and unwavering devotion.

Ecclesiastes.

VIII.

CHAPTERS X. 10—XII. 1.

IN contrasting the self-effacement of wise men with the self-assertiveness of fools, Koheleth has told us that wise men will always recognise and submit to the force of circumstances. Fools, on the other hand, recognise nothing but their own wishes and whims. They will often make a futile resistance to an almost omnipotent despot—a resistance which results only in their own ruin. This subject he continues in verse 10.

A wise man knows what he is about; he knows how to adapt his means to ends, or at any rate how to estimate his means. He knows that if the axe be blunt, he must put forth more strength than would otherwise be necessary, and that consequently there will be a waste of energy. Wisdom teaches a man to sharpen his axe, or, in other words, to employ sagacity and *finesse* rather than mere brute force. The serpent will sting, unless he is charmed; mere babbling is of no avail. [Instead of "a babbler is no better," as in our version, we should read, There is no profit, no use, in a babbler.] From time immemorial in Egypt, Syria, Persia and India, there has been, as you know, a class of persons who manage to gain a power over snakes, so that they can draw them from their retreats, handle them with impunity, and make them follow their footsteps like dogs. This power is, really or ostensibly, connected with certain muttered words and certain peculiar intonations of the voice. Mere babbling, says Koheleth, will never charm the snakes. Just so is it in political life. Verbosity is not eloquence. The words of a wise man win him favour, but the lips of a fool swallow up himself. The wise man talks so persuasively as to conciliate even the despot; but a fool ruins himself by his foolish talk. He will bore you when he seeks to be amusing; he will insult you when he tries to pay a compliment; he will injure every project which he takes in hand to support; he will make enemies for himself just in proportion as he tries to make friends. From beginning to end his words are madness;—and it is, unfortunately, a long time before the end is reached. He is everlastingly talking. Though no man knoweth what shall be here nor what shall be hereafter, yet the fool will talk glibly about it. He will give you lengthy disquisitions even upon the profoundest mysteries of existence. Like Bunyan's Mr Talkative, he will discourse of things heavenly, or of things earthly; of thing moral, or of things evangelical; of things sacred, or of things profane; of things past, or of things to come; of things foreign, or of things at home; of things more essential, or of things circumstantial. All the little energy he possesses he spends in talk; and any genuine work that he has to perform he finds fatiguing. The labour of a fool is wearisome to him, says Koheleth; he does not even know the way to the city. This is a proverbial expression for very dense ignorance and stupidity. The Jews said of the man of business that he knew his way to the city, just as we say of the man of fashion that he knows his way about town. The fool, Koheleth means to say, has no notion of business.

In verse 16 he mentions an instance, in which

the fool's want of common-sense would most likely be apparent—in which he would very probably blurt out something to his own ruin. It is unfortunate, Koheleth admits, when the king is childish and the princes luxurious. [That is the meaning of eating in the morning—commencing the day with festivity instead of work.] By the slothfulness or negligence of such princes the building decayeth—that is, the whole fabric of the state falls into ruin. In verse 19, instead of "A feast is made for laughter, and wine maketh merry; but money answereth all things," we should read—They make themselves merry with feasts and wine-parties, and the money (of the people, or some such phrase understood) ministers to their inclinations. In other words, their debaucheries are carried on with the money they have extorted from their subjects. The hiatus may have been left for two reasons. Koheleth may have been afraid of giving offence by his strictures to some existing ruler; or he may have wished to show his readers that he could practise what, in the next verse, he proceeds to preach —viz., the virtue of silence. Nevertheless, he continues, in spite of all the evils arising from misgovernment—nevertheless, curse not the king. Do not say anything against him, not even in your bed-chamber. If you do, be sure it will come to his ears. It will seem as if the very birds listened, and repeated what they saw. In despotic governments the system of espionage is sometimes carried so far, that there ceases to be any such thing as privacy. The origin of the proverb about the bird's love of scandal I explained before.[1]

In chapter xi. Koheleth urges upon us the necessity of diligence. He has come to the conclusion that it is not worth while to have a nicely calculated scheme of life; because, at every turn, our calculations may be upset by the interference of an arbitrary Providence. But on the other hand, as he now points out, we must do *something*, or we shall have no enjoyment at all. We shall never reap, if we do not sow. And we must be prepared to work, he tells us, even when there is no immediate prospect of reward. We must be ready even to throw away our labour, " to cast our bread upon the waters." This is a proverbial expression for a useless or thankless task, corresponding to the Greek σπείρειν ἐπὶ πόντῳ.

A very important part of our work in life consists, Koheleth says, in making friends. We

[1] Note, p. 170.

may be prosperous—so prosperous as to fancy we can do without them; and yet he advises us "to give a portion to seven, and even to eight"—to be generous to a large number of people. For, as he acutely adds, you know not what evil shall be upon earth: you are prosperous now, but calamity may come to you at any moment. If it does, your generosity will be requited; your gifts, which seem to be wasted—as much wasted as if you had flung them into the stream—"you will find again after many days." These words are often quoted as if they referred to a really Christian charity. It is evident, however, that Koheleth is merely recommending us to give, hoping to receive as much, or more, again. And we know what Christ thought of that kind of generosity. We know how contemptuously he asked, "do not even the Pharisees—the hypocrites—the same?" We know that

> "Heaven disdains the lore
> Of nicely calculated less and more."

In the third and following verses, he warns us against being misled by a doctrine, on which he has previously much insisted—the doctrine, viz., that we never know what God is going to do with us. You remember he has told us, more than once that our best laid schemes, our most carefully elaborated plans, might be suddenly frustrated, by some unexpected and inexplicable interference on the part of Providence. But now he tells us that, though this is an argument against our forming too elaborate a programme of life, it must not be allowed to keep us from a moderate amount of industry. We must do what we have to do *in spite of* our short-sightedness. We should never do anything at all, if we waited till we could see into futurity. For example, as he says, we have no scientific knowledge of meteorology. We cannot forecast the weather. The wind is detrimental to our sowing, and the rain to our reaping. But we cannot tell when the wind or rain will come. All we know, he ironically observes, is, that if the clouds are full of rain, they will empty themselves upon the earth; and that, when the wind has blown down a tree, there the tree has to lie—the wind won't blow it up again. In other words, all we know is, that it blows when it blows, and that it rains when it rains.[1]

---

[1] Koheleth's remark reminds one of Goethe's verse :—
   " Es regnet was es regnet will
   Und regnet seine Lauf;
   Und wenn es nicht mehr regnen will,
   Dann hört es wieder auf."

If we only began to sow, when we were certain the wind would not get up; if we only began to reap, when we were certain the clouds would not arise,—we should never sow or reap at all. We are as ignorant of "the work of God"—that is, of the ways of Providence—as we are of the manner in which the framework of the body is built up. We cannot possibly foresee how God is going to treat us. But this after all, Koheleth says, is an argument for industry rather than for sloth. In the morning sow thy seed, and in the evening withhold not thy hand—that is, be diligent all the day long [the morning and evening, the two ends of the day, denoting the whole of it]; for thou knowest not whether shall prosper either this or that, or whether they both shall be alike good. Some of our efforts may fail; but on the other hand all may succeed. It is worth while therefore to be diligent, *on the chance* that our diligence may be rewarded. Koheleth seems to be afraid that his readers, if they accept his doctrine of Providence, may throw up the game of life in despair. But he says in effect: Come, I did not mean you to do that. Things are not so bad after all. Providence may thwart you; but it may assist you. If you do nothing, you are sure to be miserable; if you do some-

s

thing, you *may* enjoy yourself: therefore work. It is no good throwing away that life of yours. The light is sweet, and it is a pleasant thing for the eyes to behold the sun. Instead of wasting your existence, rather try to crowd into it all the enjoyment that you can.

However much pleasure you may have had, do not relax in your efforts after more. Remember the days of darkness, for they shall be many. All that is coming is vanity. The undiscovered country is at best but a land of shadows. Think of the eternal grave, and let the thought induce you to make the best of the present life. It is your only chance.—The anticipation of death has often been similarly used as a stimulus to pleasure. It was on this principle that a coffin, containing the figure of a corpse, was carried round at the Egyptian banquets. "Look at this," said the bearer to each of the guests; "you will one day be like it, therefore drink and be merry." Young man, says Koheleth, enjoy yourself in your youth. Make the most of that golden season. Walk in the ways of thine heart and in the sight of thine eyes. Indulge your inclinations, so far as you safely can.

Only you must remember not to overdo it, not to be overmuch wicked. Recollect that for all these things God will bring you into judgment. God always punishes excess. Seek pleasure, but avoid sensuality. Remove sorrow from your heart and put away evil from your flesh: that is to say, on the one hand eschew melancholy, go in for gaiety and enjoyment; but on the other hand, beware of over-indulgence, which entails such terrible penalties on the flesh. Youth and manhood are vanity; they are fast passing away. And in old age you will reap what you have previously sown. Remember, therefore, thy Creator in the days of thy youth. Bethink you, before it is too late, of those natural laws, which cannot be broken with impunity.

Just notice, if you please, the contrast between this worldly philosophy of Koheleth's and the Jewish religion at its best. I don't know whether or not he was aware of the fact, but the precept which he here enunciates is distinctly contrary to one which we find in the Pentateuch (Numbers xv. 39). There we read, "Seek *not* after your own heart and your own eyes; but remember to do all the commandments of the Lord, and be holy unto your God." Koheleth says, on the contrary,—Walk in the ways of thine heart and in the sight of thine eyes; only remember to do so with a certain amount of care, inasmuch as a reckless indulgence will inevitably lead to pain. In other words, according to Judaism, God, righteousness, holiness, character, stand first; and to them our personal inclinations must be altogether subordinated. According to Koheleth, pleasure stands first. God is introduced only as an after-thought or a check. He has attached certain punishments to certain forms of pleasure, and these forms of pleasure are therefore to be avoided. Obeying the commandments of God, according to Judaism, is something highly positive; it is the achievement of a holy character. Obeying the commandments of God, according to Koheleth, is something purely negative; it only means abstaining from those vices which are sure not to pay. According to Judaism, God is an object of adoration, on account of His goodness. "As the heart panteth after the water-brooks, so panteth my soul after Thee, O God." "O Lord, what love have I unto Thy law; it is my meditation all the day." Communion with God was felt, by the really pious Jew, to be the supreme happiness of life. But, according to Koheleth, God is to be obeyed merely because He will punish disobedience.

If we look around us to-day, we shall find that there are still two kinds of morality and two kinds of religion—the one real, the other only spurious and nominal. Some men are spiritual enough to see beauty in goodness, and to love it for its own sake; others care for it only as it brings them profit. Some recoil from evil with an instinctive loathing; others would prefer it to goodness, if it but paid as well. There are some whose sole aim is self-advancement: for this they will deny themselves, but for nothing else. There are others whose first and chief desire is to live truly and nobly; who are willing to sacrifice pleasure for duty, their own interests for the interests of others; and who are ready, if the welfare of humanity may be advanced thereby, to lay down their very lives. And just as we find a spurious morality, a morality that is nothing but worldliness, so we find a spurious religion, a religion that is nothing but "other-worldliness." Just as men often act virtuously from vicious motives, so do they often act religiously from irreligious motives. They fancy they are serving God, when they are only serving themselves. They will go to church, and receive the sacrament, and believe in Christ, and so forth, merely to escape the flames of hell. If Satan were the strongest power in the universe, they would be equally ready to do as much for him. They have chosen God for their master, merely because He gives better wages than the devil.

Now, true morality is devotion of the soul to goodness; true religion is devotion of the soul to God;—devotion that is not increased by the hope of profit, nor diminished by the certainty of loss. You have an example of genuine morality in Socrates, whose love of truth enabled him to brave universal sneers and scowls. "I will venture," he said, "to be true to my convictions, though all the world oppose." You have an example of genuine religion in the Apostles, who "counted it all joy that they were thought worthy to suffer shame for Christ." If we would be true to the manhood with which we have been endowed, we too must cultivate this spirit of self-abandoning devotion to goodness and to God. We must learn to act from unselfish motives. We must examine our conduct in the light of duty, rather than of expediency. We must become supremely anxious regarding the question, "Is it right?" and almost indifferent regarding the question, "Will it pay?" And for God, the impersonation of goodness, we must conceive an attachment altogether independent of rewards and punishments. We must feel attracted to Him, not by the largeness of His resources, but by the sweetness of His character. We must think of Him as the eternal Father, who is working through the ages, amid much seeming discord and confusion, for the final good of all sentient creatures and for the ultimate perfection of all moral beings. Our hearts must kindle with enthusiasm at the thought of co-operating with Him in His transcendent work. And to this task we must devote ourselves with such singleness of purpose, that our life, losing its pettiness and isolation, shall become part of the very life of God.

Ecclesiastes.

IX.

CHAPTER XII. 1-8.

WE parted from Koheleth when he was uttering the well-known words—" Remember thy Creator in the days of thy youth." Various associations have probably led to our regarding this sentence as an expression of fervent piety. But a study of the context shows that it is nothing of the kind. All that Koheleth means is this — We are to avoid such an excessive indulgence in pleasure, as will be sure to end in excessive pain. Enjoyment, he has repeatedly told us, is our best and wisest aim. But he reminds us that the Creator's laws render a certain amount of self-control indispensable, for him who would avoid the Creator's punishments. Though Koheleth's morality is not high, and though his religion is very low, he wishes it to be understood that he has no intention of encouraging profligacy. He seems rather afraid, now that he is bringing his book to a close, lest his recommendation of enjoyment should be too warmly followed—lest it should lead his disciples into what he calls "overmuch wickedness"; and he therefore gives a graphic picture of the horror of that premature decay, which results from a reckless course of dissipation. He does so under the metaphor of a storm.

Understood in this sense the passage, which extends from the beginning of the second to the end of the fifth verse, is one of much beauty and power. It becomes however extremely grotesque, if interpreted anatomically and physiologically; and this is what most of the commentators have persisted in doing. I will just mention one or two of their explanations, in order that you may see what havoc is sometimes made by the would-be critics who are destitute of the critical faculty. The sun, the moon and the stars, have been taken to mean the forehead, the nose, the cheeks. The clouds returning after rain are supposed to signify the effects of a bad influenza. The keepers of the house are the ribs; the men of power, the thighs; the grinders, the teeth;

the women looking out of the windows, the eyes. The door being closed on the street signifies that the pores of the skin have ceased to act. The noise of the mill growing faint means that the mastication of the food becomes imperfect. The locust becoming a burden is equivalent to the swelling of the ankles. The silver cord is the backbone; the golden bowl is the brain; the bucket is the right ventricle of the heart; and the wheel that draws the water represents the lungs, because they draw in the air. Now we may be quite sure that whatever Koheleth meant, or did not mean, he could never have intended such nonsense as this. The passage is not a figurative description of the dissolution of the body, as may be readily seen by the grotesqueness of all the interpretations which assume that it is. It sets forth the threatening approach of death under the image of a tempest.

"The sun, the moon and the stars are darkened." The storm is supposed to have been gathering all day, and so the sun was obscured; and now, although the sun has set, neither moon nor stars are visible. "The clouds return after rain." There has been a good deal of rain already; but the clouds, instead of dispersing, gather anew, and pour out their contents in a perfect deluge. The fury of the storm strikes terror into the various members of the Eastern household. The keepers tremble, and the men of power shudder [literally, "writhe"]. The keepers of the house are the menial servants, whose business it is to guard the premises against robbers and marauders; the men of power are their lordly and aristocratic masters.

The grinding-maids will stop grinding because they are few, and the ladies who have been looking out of the window will be shrouded in darkness. A mill formed a most important and indispensable item in oriental housekeeping. There were no public mills; and in the warm climate the bread dried up so quickly, that it was necessary to grind and bake daily. The grinding was generally done in the evening; and the noise, arising from the simultaneous performance of it in a large number of houses, was very great. This noise is sometimes referred to in the Bible as indicative of an active and happy populace. For instance (Jeremiah xxv. 10), "I will take from them the voice of mirth, the voice of the bridegroom and the voice of the bride, and the sound of the millstones." And again (Rev. xviii. 21-23)—"That great city Babylon shall be thrown down, and the voice of harpers and musicians and pipers and trumpeters shall be heard no more at all in thee; and the voice of the bridegroom and the bride shall be heard no more at all in thee; and no craftsmen shall be found in thee; and the sound of the millstone shall be heard no more at all in thee." A sudden cessation of the mills, such as Koheleth describes, would be as striking as the stoppage of the ordinary traffic and bustle in Cheapside or Regent Street. The meaning of the grinding-maids stopping "because they are few," seems to be, that the majority of them would be terrified and run away from their work, and the few who had the courage to remain would be insufficient to carry on the process. The women employed at the mill were generally slaves—often captives taken in war. The persons referred to in the last clause of the verse, on the other hand, are the ladies of the house, whose favourite amusement was looking out of the window. This in fact, in the East, was about the only amusement permitted them. They are here represented as shrouded in darkness — that is, they are so alarmed at the violence of the storm, that they go away from the windows, and retire into the innermost rooms of the establishment.

Thus all the members of the household, masters and servants, mistresses and maids, are described as being thrown into a state of the greatest consternation. No sooner had the noise of the grinding ceased, than there would be a rush to the doors, which would be bolted and barred, so as to keep out as much of the rain and wind as possible. The last half of verse 4 is entirely wrong in our version. Instead of, "He shall rise up at the voice of the bird, and all the daughters of music shall be brought low," it should be,—The swallow rises to shriek, and the singing birds retire. The swallow loves the wind and the tempest, and he therefore shrieks for joy. The delicate song-birds, on the contrary, are frightened, and hurry to the shelter of their nests. In verse 5, instead of, "The almond-tree shall flourish, and the grasshopper shall be a burden, and desire shall fail," we should read,—The almond shall be despised, and the locust shall be loathed, and the caperberry shall be powerless. The people are so alarmed at "the storm which is coming from on high and the terrors which are on their way," that all the delicacies of the table lose their charm. Both almonds and locusts were favourite articles of diet in the East, and the caperberry was used as a provocative to appetite. Sir Henry Rawlinson tells us that at the present day the gourmands of Persia will sit for hours before dinner eating fruit and drinking wine, and trying in various ways to create an appetite. But now at the approach of the storm even the epicure can think of nothing but his fears. You must remember that thunderstorms are comparatively rare in Syria and the adjacent countries; and this of course makes them appear all the more alarming. Throughout the Old Testament we find many traces of the dread which these storms inspired,—as, for instance, in the graphic description of the tempest at the close of the Book of Job.

Now this terror which he has described so vividly, Koheleth says, is a parable,—a parable of the dismay that falls upon the sensualist, when he discovers that his constitution has been shattered and that death is approaching, when he is about to set forth to his long home and the mourners are going about the streets. The long home, or more literally "the house of eternity," was, and is still, a Jewish synonym for the grave. The horror of dying is increased by the fact, graphically alluded to by Koheleth, that the professional mourners may sometimes be seen loitering under the windows of the expiring man, in the hope that they may be hired to lament him; or going about hither and thither for the purpose of gathering information, which they will afterwards introduce into a funeral dirge.

Koheleth lingers over the description and works it up thus elaborately, because he is anxious to warn us against "overmuch wickedness"; and he uses the storm as a metaphor, to symbolise the terrible kind of death which comes to the reckless sensualist. Remember thy Creator, he says, in the days of thy youth. It will be too late in the evil days when life is altogether destitute of pleasure. The evil days spoken of here, you will observe, are not the days of old age as such, but of the premature and diseased old age, which men create for themselves by vice. By disregarding the divine laws, says Koheleth, not only will your later life be destitute of pleasure, but it will be as full of horror as an Eastern city at the approach of a thunderstorm. Remember, therefore, thy Creator, and think of His laws, before it be too late. In verses 6 and 7 he proceeds to describe death in other terms, so that the advice he is offering may have a wider scope. Death may come more suddenly than a tempest; it may come instantaneously without any warning. The metaphors in verse 6 are intended to symbolise this kind of death. Remember thy Creator, he says, before the silver cord be snapped or the golden bowl broken, before the pitcher be broken at the fountain or the wheel at the cistern. It was customary, both with the Hebrews and Greeks, to represent life under the figure of a lamp, and also under the figure of a fountain. In this passage Koheleth describes the lamp of life as being destroyed, through the snapping of the cord by which it was suspended; and he represents the fountain of life as being rendered useless, through the breaking of the wheel by means of which the water was to be extracted. Just as these things happen suddenly and unexpectedly in your everyday experience, so death, he says, may come to you suddenly and unexpectedly. Therefore, remember your Creator while you can. But even if death did not come in horror, even if it did not come suddenly, come at last it must, and therefore he adds in verse 7 a final clause which is universally applicable. Remember thy Creator before [not "then," as in our version] the body returns to the earth as it was, and the spirit returns to God who gave it. What he means by this we shall see in the next sermon. That he was not thinking of immortality is proved by the fact that he immediately adds, "Vanity of vanities, all is vanity." The return of our spirit to God, Koheleth thinks, is but an unsatisfactory conclusion to a life that has been throughout unsatisfactory. Remember thy Creator, he insists; and yet in the same breath he asks, What is the good? The end of it all is vanity.

Now it is desirable that you should contrast this book of Koheleth's with the apocryphal Book of Wisdom, which latter seems to have been written for the purpose of exposing and correcting Koheleth's errors. The writer of the Book of Wisdom adopts the form of personated authorship. He too writes as Solomon, the son of David. He does not describe himself, however, as having tried the experiments of luxury, magnificence and voluptuousness; but as being an ideal sage, who had consecrated his entire life to the pursuit of goodness. This writer puts all Koheleth's favourite doctrines into the mouths of those whom he calls "the wicked" or "the scoffers." In the Book of Wisdom it is the wicked who describe human life as short and miserable. It is they who call it madness. It is the wicked who assert that we shall be hereafter as though we had never been; that death and

T

life are determined by chance; that our body will finally be turned into ashes and our spirit vanish into soft air; and that beyond the grave there is nothing but oblivion awaiting us. It is the wicked who say, Let us enjoy the good things that are present, let us fill ourselves with costly wine and ointment. In the Book of Wisdom Koheleth is over and over again contradicted point-blank. For example, in reply to his assertion that he never succeeded in finding a single good woman, the writer of the Book of Wisdom observes sarcastically, that those who despise wisdom must expect to have foolish wives. And in reply to the assertion that the wise man dieth as the fool, the writer of the Book of Wisdom remarks, that it is only in the sight of the unwise that he seems to die.

It may appear strange that Ecclesiastes, which is so full of error, should have been admitted into the Sacred Canon; and that the Book of Wisdom, the doctrine of which is at once more wholesome and more orthodox, should have been excluded. How it happened I do not know. But there is this to be said in favour of Ecclesiastes,—Koheleth was a far abler man, and therefore a far more suggestive writer, than the author of the Book of Wisdom. It is true that the latter assumes immortality; but I venture to say, no man's faith in another existence was ever strengthened by a perusal of the Book of Wisdom. It is true that Ecclesiastes denies immortality; but the philosophy of life which it constructs on the basis of this denial, is so mean, so ghastly, so repellent, that we are startled into reflection. We involuntarily say to ourselves—If the denial of immortality leads to such conclusions as Koheleth's, may not, must not, that denial be erroneous?

As I pointed out to you last Advent, immortality is the essential basis of real religion.[1] Many modern scientists who disbelieve in immortality are men of the highest moral tone, and, according to the author of 'Natural Religion,' men of genuine piety. But *logically* they have no business to be so. Logically there is but one philosophy consistent with the denial of a future life, and that is the philosophy of Koheleth. And now that the disbelief in immortality is spreading with great rapidity, it seems to me worth our while to make a careful study of this book of Ecclesiastes, where the corollaries of such a disbelief are deduced for us by an acute and consistent thinker.

[1] See note, p. 3.

At first, you remember, I spoke of two or three sermons upon the subject; but they have grown, you see, into three times three. The fact is, it was only after I began to study the book myself, with the view of assisting you in your study of it—it was only then that I discovered the difficulty of the task I had set myself. Our Authorised Version is particularly inaccurate and misleading; and I soon saw it would be impossible to explain what I conceived to be Koheleth's meaning, unless I said something about almost every verse. To many congregations I should probably have apologised for having lingered over the subject so long. To you I think I need not apologise. You know—or perhaps you do not know—that a preacher criticises his congregation, just as his congregation criticises him. It has been my happiness to preach to you for almost four years, and I have come to look upon the most of you as fellow-students. Now the first law of a student's life is completeness. He feels that he must master every subject he undertakes as fully and perfectly as possible. However, it is satisfactory even for a student to bring his task to a conclusion; and therefore I am pleased to tell you, all that remains to be said upon Ecclesiastes I shall say next Sunday.

Ecclesiastes.

X.

CHAPTER XII. 9-14.

THE book of Ecclesiastes ends, as it begins, with the words, "Vanity of vanities, all is vanity." That sentence is its theme. Anything else the book contains, occurs only incidentally and illustratively.

Verses 9-14 constitute an epilogue or postscript. They were written by some other hand. For, firstly, the writer of the postscript speaks in the third person. He says,—the Preacher was, or did, so and so. But Koheleth always speaks of himself in the first: he says,—I, the Preacher, was, or did, so and so. Secondly, the writer of the postscript is more orthodox than the writer of the book; inasmuch as he represents the fear of God to be the conclusion of the whole matter.

But, as we have seen, with Koheleth this fear of God came in only as a part of prudence. Koheleth does not exhort us to consecrate ourselves to the service of God with unreserved devotion. On the contrary, he exhorts us to devote ourselves to pleasure, and he introduces the fear of God merely as a necessary check, to keep us from "the overmuch wickedness," which is inevitably followed by a terrible retribution. Thirdly, we find in verse 14 a reference to a system of universal retribution, in which, Koheleth tells us over and over again, he does not believe.

As to the subject-matter of the postscript:— verse 9 informs us that Koheleth was a sage, a public teacher, and an author. He had composed many parables or stories [not "proverbs"]. Verse 10 tells us [according to the marginal reading] that he had tried to find out "words of delight." This must refer to the parables, and not to the work before us; for no more depressing book than Ecclesiastes was ever composed since the world began. The latter part of the postscript, however, which asserts that he wrote down the words of truth with uprightness, will apply to the present treatise. Honesty is our author's great charm. He tells us exactly what he thinks and feels, even when he must know we shall not respect him very much for his pains.

In verses 11 and 12 we have a few remarks on literature in general. Verse 11 should read —The words of the wise are like goads, and those of the masters of assemblies are like fixed stakes, provided by the same shepherd. The meaning is this,—Just as the same shepherd will sometimes employ goads, to drive his sheep on to fresh pastures, and at other times will employ stakes, in order to keep them within the old ones, so the words of the wise which lead onwards, propounding new truth (what we should call liberal or Broad Church thought), and the words of the masters of assemblies which keep to the old truth (what we should call orthodox or evangelical thought), proceed from the same source and have one common object. "Masters of assemblies" was a technical name for the heads of those colleges and schools, which during the rabbinical period were to be found in every town and almost every hamlet of Judæa. The same man might of course, and commonly did, bear both titles—the master of an assembly being most frequently one who had previously acquired a reputation as a sage. The meaning of the passage is that truth and right are not confined to any party. The Broad Churchman who is progressive, the Evangelical who is stationary, may both be trying their best, though in diametrically opposite ways, to benefit those committed to their charge. In verse 12, instead of "Further, by these, my son, be admonished," we should read,—And beyond these, my son, beware; that is, avoid all other kinds of reading: for of making many books there is no end, and much reading is a weariness to the flesh. Read only, the writer means, the books of the wise. Don't tire yourself, and don't waste your time, over worthless literature. This corresponds somewhat to the advice of Marcus Aurelius, "Free yourself from the thirst for books:" advice which it might be well to repeat in the present day, when so many persons are in the habit of pouring into their minds fifth-rate three-volume novels by the gross.

In verses 13 and 14 we have a short system of ethics—a summary of human duty, and the consequences of its neglect. But, as I have said, Koheleth would not have agreed to it. If it is intended, therefore, as an exposition of his views, it is not correct. If, on the other hand, it is intended as an exposition of the views of the epilogist or writer of the postscript, we see that he must have been a more religious man than the author of Ecclesiastes. In any case it could not have been written by Koheleth himself.

It now remains for me to explain to you, what it was that Koheleth meant by the spirit returning to God. As I have said already, it is clear that he was not thinking of immortality, or he would not have added immediately afterwards, "Vanity of vanities, all is vanity." We need not be surprised at Koheleth's disbelief in immortality, for we find among the Jews men infinitely better, infinitely more spiritual than he, who had never even dreamed of it. The absence of any allusion to a future life, in some of the books of the Old Testament, is almost startling. For example, in the 26th chapter of Leviticus and the 28th chapter of Deuteronomy, all sorts of blessings are pronounced on those who keep the law, and all sorts of curses invoked on those who break it; but there is not the slightest hint that a man's conduct will have any effect upon his condition after death. When the sceptics of those days asserted that the servants of the Lord were sometimes in adversity, and that therefore it was of no use to serve Him, the orthodox invariably answered them by maintaining, that matters would be satisfactorily rectified in the present life. It would be well with the righteous sooner or later (they said) *here;* it would not be well with the wicked in the end *here.* No reference was made to any difference in their condition hereafter. Take, for example, the 37th Psalm : " Fret not thyself because of evil-doers, for evil-doers shall be cut off. Those that wait upon the Lord shall inherit the earth. Wait on the Lord and keep His way, and He shall exalt thee to inherit the earth : when the wicked are cut off, thou shalt see it. I have seen the wicked in great power, spreading himself like a green bay tree. Yet he passed away, and, lo, he was not. Mark the perfect man, and behold the upright: for the end of that man is peace." So too the prophets, though they were never tired of speaking of a future reign of righteousness, seldom if ever alluded to a personal survival of the righteous.

The Jewish conception of what happened after death was very similar to that of the Greeks. The latter, you remember, did not believe exactly in annihilation. The continued existence they anticipated was something between being and not-being. Man survived only as a shadow of his former self. Intellectually and morally he ended at death. Homer speaks of life and form in Hades, but says there is *no mind* there. The joy and interest of existence were supposed then to be over for ever. There was not even the excitement of possibly dying again. The primitive Hebrew conception was, if possible, even drearier than the Greek. Sheol which, curiously enough, is rendered in our version thirty-one times " grave " and thirty-one times " hell," but which really means the place of departed souls,—Sheol was regarded by the Jews as a vast subterranean cavern, having barred and bolted gates, just like an ordinary Jewish tomb. While the departed Greeks had the power of flitting about in a certain ghostlike fashion, the Jewish shades were altogether incapable of movement. They lay like corpses in a sepulchre. No distinctions of character were recognised in this gloomy under-world. It was the common receptacle for all, good and bad. For a long time the Jews believed that Jehovah's control did not reach to Sheol. The King of Terrors was its only lord. Those who had been God's sheep when alive, in the grave would have another shepherd—viz., Death. For example, in Psalm xlix. 14 we read, "They lie in the grave like sheep; Death shall feed them" So in Psalm xlviii. 14 we read, "This God is our God for ever and ever; He will be our guide unto death." Yes, only unto death. *There* the guidance of Jehovah ceased. The inhabitants of Sheol were destitute of feeling; they passed their time in a state of sleep or coma. They were unable to hold any intercourse either with earth or heaven. Worst of all, perhaps, they were surrounded by eternal darkness. Look by way of illustration at Psalm xlix. 19, "He shall go to the generation of his fathers; they shall never see light." Or look at the still more graphic description given by Job (x. 21), where he speaks of Sheol as a "land of darkness and the shadow of death; a land of darkness, as darkness itself; and of the shadow of death, without any order, where the light is as darkness." Throughout the Old Testament, and especially in the Psalms, we find constant reference to what may be designated the non-existent existence of the dead. It is called (Psalm xxxix. 13) "being no more." "O spare me, that I may recover strength, before I go hence and be no more." Many of the Psalms were evidently written by persons in great affliction; and their complaint was the same as Job's—that their little span of existence was being wasted in calamity. Take for example the 88th Psalm, "My soul is full of trouble; it seems as if Thou hadst forgotten me. I am like the dead who lie in the grave, whom Thou rememberest no more." And then the writer proceeds to argue with God, as Job used to argue,[1] that it would soon be too late to do him any good. "Wilt Thou show wonders to the dead? Shall the dead arise and praise thee? Shall Thy loving-kindness be declared in the grave? or Thy faithfulness in destruction? Shall Thy wonders be known in the dark? or Thy righteousness in the land of forgetfulness?" We find the same view even in a prophet like Isaiah (xxxviii. 18): "The grave cannot praise Thee, death cannot celebrate Thee."

One or two of the psalmists, however, were gifted in an extraordinary degree with "the vision and faculty divine;" and to them the thought of immortality was revealed. They loved God with such a passionate devotion, and the idea of being cut off from communion with Him seemed so terrible, that gradually they became convinced nothing could ever effect this

[1] See my 'Defects of Modern Christianity, and other Sermons,' pp. 99 and 104.

dread separation, not even death itself. The Book of Psalms contains three (and but three) verses which imply a belief in immortality,—" Thou wilt not leave my soul in hell; neither wilt Thou suffer Thine Holy One to see corruption" (xvi. 10). "God will redeem my soul from the power of the grave; for He shall receive me" (xlix. 15). "Thou shalt guide me by Thy council, and afterwards receive me to glory" (lxxiii. 24). The prophet Hosea too seems to have reached the same spiritual vision (xiii. 14): "I will ransom them from the power of the grave; I will redeem them from death: O death, I will be thy plagues; O grave, I will be thy destruction." Such outbursts of inspiration however were very rare, and had, at the time, no effect upon the popular belief.

Now the idea of immortality, which but seldom flashed across the minds even of psalmists and seers, was not likely to occur to such a man as Koheleth. Five times he tells us in his short treatise that there is nothing better in life than enjoyment (ii. 24, iii. 12, v. 18, viii. 15, ix. 7). He never retracts this view. The very righteousness which he preached is no more than expediency. He urges us to remember the Creator, because, if we do not, we shall suffer for it. Had he believed in immortality, he would have been a much better man; or, at any rate, he would have written a much better book. By the spirit returning to God, he means just what the Jews of his time would have meant. They distinguished between the spirit and the soul. The spirit was a comprehensive name for the whole of the higher faculties; and they regarded it as an emanation from God, or rather as a portion of the Divine Spirit. By the soul they meant merely the animal life, or principle of vitality. They considered that death, which consigned the soul to Sheol, was the signal for the re-absorption of the human spirit into the divine. The return of the spirit to God practically made an end of the individual to whom it had once belonged. Memory, conscience, will, all that goes to make up that mysterious something which we call personality, was conceived of as existing only in the union of body, soul, and spirit; and so death, which severed this connection, resulted to all intents and purposes in annihilation. No wonder that the thought of it wrung from Koheleth once more the bitter refrain—"Vanity of vanities, all is vanity." The return of the spirit to God was the last and most terrible catastrophe in the tragic drama of human life.

Hundreds of men have felt and said the same as Koheleth. I will give you two illustrations—one from oriental, and the other from English, literature. The Persian poet Omar Kayyam says, "With them"—that is, with certain sages of whom he had been speaking—

> "With them the seed of wisdom did I sow,
> And with my own hand wrought to make it grow;
> And this was all the harvest that I reaped:—
> I came like water, and like wind I go
> Into the universe; and why not knowing,
> Nor whence, like water willy nilly flowing;
> And out of it, as wind along the waste,
> I know not whither, willy nilly blowing."

Still more despairing is the cry of an English writer who once believed in immortality, but who finds himself unable any longer to do so. "I am not ashamed to confess," says the author of a 'Candid Examination of Theism,' "that [with these new views] the universe has lost its soul of loveliness; and although from henceforth the precept, 'to work while it is day,' will doubtless gain an intensified force, from the terribly intensified meaning of the words, 'the night cometh when no man can work;' yet when at times I think, as think at times I must, of the hallowed glory of that creed which once was mine, and the lonely mystery of existence as I now find it,—at such times I shall ever feel it impossible to avoid the sharpest pang of which my nature is susceptible. For whether it be due to my intelligence not being sufficiently advanced to meet the requirements of the age, or whether it be due to the memory of those sacred associations which, to me at least, were the sweetest life has given, I cannot but feel that the precept 'know thyself' has become transformed into the terrific oracle—

'Mayst thou never know the truth of what thou art.'"

Now the fact that the present life becomes contemptible when the future life is denied, is not of course, by itself, a sufficient reason for believing in immortality; but it is a reason for refusing to give up that belief except upon very cogent evidence. Mr Frederic Harrison and his school attempt to gloss over the horrors of annihilation, by dwelling upon what they call subjective immortality—that is, upon our survival in the memory of our fellow-men, and in their increasing happiness, which we had helped to further. But if we are *unconscious* of our own survival—as, according to Mr Harrison and his school, we shall be—what does it avail us? Such a survival is, for the individual, indistinguishable from annihilation. I would ask you, therefore—especially those of you who may have been influenced by the deadly spells of modern negative science—I would ask you to ponder over Koheleth's philosophy, which is a strictly logical deduction from the denial of immortality. If this life be our only life, human history is correctly summed up in the phrase, "Vanity of vanities, all is vanity." We have been dragged out of nothingness, and made to endure "the heartaches and the thousand natural ills that flesh is heir to," only to be hurled back again into nothingness at the last. We may have struggled bravely to live a useful, self-denying, heroic life, and to help on the progress of the world; but the improvement, for which we have worked, we shall never see. Long ere then we shall have been cast "as rubbish to the void."

Now I say, if we are to believe such a creed as this, we must have evidence for it little, if at all, short of certainty. And when we ask the English school of philosophers for their proofs, what do they offer us? Why, they say we cannot imagine how consciousness continues to exist after death; which piece of evidence, if it is good for anything, would disprove the present life as well as the future. We cannot imagine how consciousness exists at all. What it is, and what it depends on, we have not the faintest notion. Whereas, in favour of the doctrine of immortality, we may urge the argument, which is commonly advanced in favour of the theory of evolution—viz., it explains phenomena which are otherwise inexplicable. It solves the riddle of life. We find within ourselves a thirst for happiness, and yet we are never happy. We find within ourselves a yearning for moral perfectness, and yet we are miserably imperfect. We find within ourselves a sentiment of justice, and yet this sentiment is being for ever violated, by the fortunes and misfortunes of our neighbours. Immortality, and immortality alone, can harmonise these strange contradictions. And immortality not only solves the problem of life, but solves it satisfactorily. To Koheleth, and to those who disbelieve in a future state, our gladdest joy is but a transient ray of light, darting athwart the dismal passage to the tomb. To St Paul and those who believe in a future life, our direst affliction is but a passing cloud, as necessary to our welfare as the sunshine which for the moment it conceals; it is but one of the "all things" working together for our good—working out for us a far more exceeding and an eternal weight of glory.

THE END.

www.ingramcontent.com/pod-product-compliance
Lightning Source LLC
Chambersburg PA
CBHW022047230426
43672CB00008B/1097